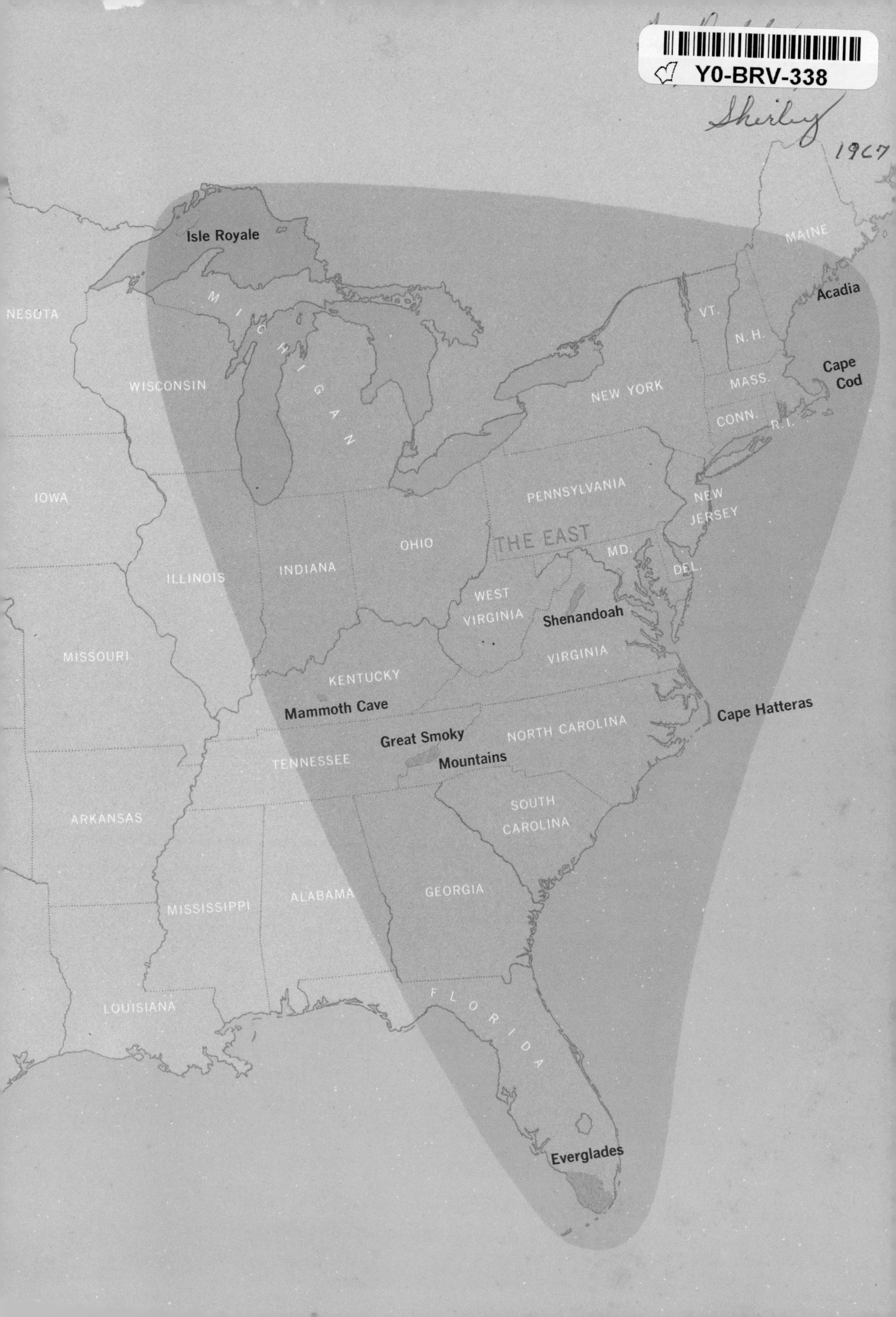

Shirley
1967
Y0-BRV-338
Isle Royale
MAINE
Acadia
NESOTA
MICHIGAN
VT.
N.H.
Cape
Cod
WISCONSIN
NEW YORK
MASS.
CONN.
R.I.
IOWA
PENNSYLVANIA
NEW
JERSEY
THE EAST
OHIO
INDIANA
MD.
ILLINOIS
DEL.
WEST
VIRGINIA
Shenandoah
MISSOURI
VIRGINIA
KENTUCKY
Mammoth Cave
Cape Hatteras
Great Smoky
Mountains
NORTH CAROLINA
TENNESSEE
SOUTH
CAROLINA
ARKANSAS
ALABAMA
GEORGIA
MISSISSIPPI
FLORIDA
LOUISIANA
Everglades

National Parks

A Guide to the National Parks and Monuments of the United States

by PAUL JENSEN

GOLDEN PRESS  NEW YORK

ACKNOWLEDGMENTS

The following people and organizations were of great assistance in preparing this book:

The National Geographic Society triggered my interest in the national parks by sending me to visit some of them as a staff member several years ago. I worked on their own book about the parks, America's Wonderlands, *for more than a year, and that was an education in itself.*

Gerald Simons, Robert Couse, David Thompson, John Kauffmann, and John Porter provided much of the text. Jim Shriner, Bill Belknap, and Nancy Wilder helped.

The National Park Service, as usual, assisted beyond any measure of duty. It is a wonderful organization and I as a citizen am proud of it. I congratulate Conrad Wirth, the Director, for maintaining what seems to me to be unusually high standards. Ralph Anderson, Miss Coiner, Wayne Replogle, and especially Merlin Potts were of particular assistance.

Finally, I want to thank my wife who helped with the interminable correspondence, and my daughter Karen, and Susan Shriner, who sometimes travel with me.

P.J.

PICTURE CREDITS

RALPH H. ANDERSON, p. 70 (top)

RAY ATKESON, pp. 31, 46, 48, 53, 56 (top), 56 (bot.), 65, 66, 71, 161

N. A. BISHOP, p. 38

DORIS BRY, p. 94

E. J. BUCKNALL, pp. 134 (bot.), 138 (top), 138 (bot.), 139 (bot.)

FLORIDA STATE NEWS BUREAU, pp. 132, 134 (top), 136 (top), 136 (bot.)

GREAT NORTHERN RAILWAY, pp. 29 (top), 30, 32

HEMLER POST CARD CO., p. 100

ALICIA HILLS, pp. 51, 52 (top & bot.)

INTERMOUNTAIN TOURIST SUPPLY CO., p. 41 (top)

JACKSON HOLE PRESERVES, pp. 26, 162, 163

PAUL JENSEN, pp. 14, 16, 20 (top), 22, 23, 39, 63, 64, 69 (bot.), 83, 88, 89, 90, 91 (top & bot.), 92, 93, 95, 109, 110-111, 114, 123, 128, 131

MERRITT E. JOHNSON, pp. 120, 121

J. M. KAUFFMAN, p. 78

HUBERT LOWMAN, p. 42

STEVE MCCUTCHEON, p. 156, 157, 158

JOSEPH MEUNCH, pp. 34-35

TOM MCHUGH, NATIONAL AUDUBON SOCIETY, p. 155

MONKMEYER PRESS PHOTO SERVICE, pp. 12, 69 (top), 79, 160 (bot.)

PHOTO RESEARCHERS, pp. 47, 107, 137, 152-153, 159, 160 (top)

JOHN P. PORTER, III, pp. 28-29

MERLIN K. POTTS, pp. 54-55, 57 (top & bot.)

RAPHO GUILLUMETTE, pp. 33 (top), 33 (bot. right), 108, 122, 130 (top)

WAYNE REPLOGLE, pp. 17 (top left & right & bot.), 18 (top & bot.), 19 (top left & bot. right), 21 (top)

HAL ROTH, pp. 74, 76, 77, 112-113

FRANK SARTWELL, p. 142 (top)

E. T. SCOYEN, ASSOC. DIR., N.P.S., p. 106 (top)

SHOSTAL, p. 62 (bot. right)

RICHARD G. SMITH, p. 147

BOB AND IRA SPRING, p. 59

UNION PACIFIC RAIL ROAD, pp. 24-25, 27 (bot.), 36-37, 40, 72, 80-81, 84-85, 86-87, 96-97

UTAH STATE TOURIST AND PUBLICITY AGENCY, p. 164

YOSEMITE PARK AND CURRY CO., pp. 67, 68

DEW YOUNG, p. 58

The following pictures were supplied by The National Park Service:

BADLANDS NATIONAL MONUMENT, p. 43

BIG BEND NATIONAL PARK, pp. 102, 103, 104 (top & bot.), 105

CANYON DE CHELLY NATIONAL MONUMENT, pp. 126, 127

CAPE HATTERAS NATIONAL SEASHORE RECREATIONAL AREA, pp. 148, 149

CRATERS OF THE MOON NATIONAL MONUMENT, p. 33 (bot. left)

DEATH VALLEY NATIONAL MONUMENT, p. 99

EVERGLADES NATIONAL PARK, p. 135 (top & bot.)

GLACIER NATIONAL PARK, cover, pp. 4-5

GRAND TETON NATIONAL PARK, p. 27 (top)

GREAT SMOKY MOUNTAINS NATIONAL PARK, pp. 140, 141, 142 (bot), 143 (left & right)

ISLE ROYALE NATIONAL PARK, pp. 144, 145

JOSHUA TREE NATIONAL MONUMENT, p. 107 (top)

LASSEN VOLCANIC NATIONAL PARK, pp. 41 (bot. left), 60, 61 (top & bot.), 62 (top & bot. left)

MAMMOTH CAVE NATIONAL PARK, p. 151

NAVAJO NATIONAL MONUMENT, p. 124, 125

OLYMPIC NATIONAL PARK, p. 50

RAINBOW BRIDGE NATIONAL MONUMENT, p. 7

ROCKY MOUNTAIN NATIONAL PARK, p. 38 (bot.)

SHENANDOAH NATIONAL PARK, p. 139 (top)

SUNSET CRATER NATIONAL MONUMENT, p. 129

WALNUT CANYON NATIONAL MONUMENT, p. 130 (bot.)

WIND CAVE NATIONAL PARK, p. 44, 45

YELLOWSTONE NATIONAL PARK, pp. 15, 19 (top right & bot. left), 20 (bot.), 21 (bot.)

MAPS BY ELMER SMITH PAINTING ON PP. 116-117 BY ANDRÉ DURENCEAU

Library of Congress Catalog Card Number 64-10306.

Designed and produced by Artists and Writers Press, Inc. Printed in the U.S.A. by Western Printing and Lithographing Company. Published by Golden Press, Inc., New York. Published simultaneously in Canada by The Musson Book Company, Ltd., Toronto.

Table of Contents

Utah's Rainbow Bridge was cut by a meandering stream.

Introduction

SOME OF THE MOST profound and enduring pleasures of life are to be found in the delight of a splendid landscape, and in the enjoyment of a sincere and charming love affair with nature's glories. People have always found joy in the sight of a great mountain, a stand of straight old trees, a clear stream, a green valley, a lonely beach. Primitives placed their gods in such settings—and little wonder, for there is true awesomeness in a patch of the earth where nature alone reigns.

American pioneers moving westward found magnificent scenery by the thousands of square miles. They gazed and fell in love. They saw in each vista an answer to their dreams. And they grabbed what they could for themselves, trying to wrench their dreams out of the land. Trees meant lumber, streams meant gold, valleys meant grazing. Gradually, without meaning to, Americans despoiled a good deal of what they found.

But sometimes thoughtful men determined to save a place in all its original beauty. In 1870 such an event occurred when a group of western explorers camped in the northwest corner of the newly established territory of Wyoming. The men had been marveling at the region they were in, where a river rushed through a bright canyon, where a strange pool bubbled with steam, and geysers suddenly shot into the air. They sat around the campfire swapping ideas about how they would claim and divide up this magnificent country among themselves.

A certain Judge Cornelius Hedges of Montana startled the group with an appeal to turn the whole place over to the federal government so everyone in the United States could be free to come and visit it. A pretty fanciful idea in those days, but it actually was not original with this group. Yosemite, eight years earlier, had already been set aside as a preserve to be administered by the State of California. Wyoming, however, was not yet a state and the Judge and his friends agreed that this yellowstone country ought to become a national park. For two years they fought hard for their plan, writing articles and appealing to

Olympic National Park has 50 miles of wild coastline.

Congress. Such was their influence that Yellowstone National Park was established in 1872—"a pleasuring ground," they called it—the first of its kind in the world.

Early problems of maintenance caused many a headache. Yellowstone and the other parks that followed it were put under civilian control. Then in an effort to stop poaching and other abuses, the Army guarded the parks for some thirty years. In 1916 the National Park Service was formed, a branch of the Department of the Interior. This gave the growing number of parks professional attention by men trained to the job.

If you have visited national parks you have probably seen signs or notices referring to Mission 66. This is a program which will be completed in 1966 (the park service's 50th anniversary), and will bring park facilities up to date. They need it. Judge Hedges' idea, back in 1870, touched off a tremendous public response. Visitors flocked to Yellowstone even in days of Indian troubles and stagecoach hold-ups. They crowded into Yosemite in high-riding horse-drawn carriages and hitched them to logs in the parking area. They rode a special branch of a great railroad to get to Grand Canyon. By the 1950's traffic jams were common deep in the wilderness, and tourists were being turned away from the parks because lodges, cabins, and campgrounds were overflowing.

Mission 66 enlarges accommodations for overnight visitors and builds visitor centers which explain the outstanding natural features. It constructs roads and trails, and removes unsightly buildings which interfere with the views.

The National Park Service takes care of about 25,000,000 acres of land, including parks, national monuments, recreation areas, and sites of historical interest. National parks are established by acts of Congress. They are selected because the scenic values they offer are very great, and because each has one or two special features that cannot be duplicated anywhere else. Only Yellowstone, for example, has such an array of geysers and boiling springs. Only Everglades has such a profusion of tropical life.

National monuments are established by simple proclamation by the President. In 1906 Theodore Roosevelt sought a way to protect the archeological discoveries in the Southwest – ancient pueblos and cliff dwellings. So the Antiquities Act was passed which gave him the right to set up national monuments. These areas are not necessarily smaller than the parks. Katmai National Monument in Alaska, with 2½ million acres, is the largest holding in all the park system. But the monuments do tend to be more specialized, to have a single distinct feature—an Indian ruin, an outcropping of petrified wood, a cave, a volcanic formation—that helps you learn more about the geologic or historical heritage of your country.

This book describes 27 scenic national parks. It attempts to emphasize, in each case, those values that are unique to each park in the hope that you will easily distinguish between these many glorious places, associating with each one the things that make it famous.

Here also are described 22 national monuments, chosen because they add significance to the history or geology of the land. Some of these should be, perhaps will become, parks. Seven of the national monuments are lumped together because they tell the fascinating story of the pre-Columbian Pueblo Indians whose culture reached considerable heights in the canyons and mesas of the Southwest.

Lake Mead National Recreation Area and Cape Hatteras National Seashore Recreational Area, both part of the National Park System, are also included because they fill out the story of these millions of acres that you own. They typify recreational areas designed especially for activities such as boating, water skiing, surf fishing, and swimming.

Not that there aren't plenty of activities at the parks and monuments. But often tourists become so engrossed in just plain sight-seeing that they fail to take full advantage of them.

Americans have a national tendency to travel fast and far on their vacations, pausing only briefly to sample the places they visit. The National Park Service understands this and won't be hurt if you simply drive through Yosemite, for example, and then hurry on to Sequoia and Kings Canyon. But the facilities and activities at any park are designed for leisurely, thorough visits. Stay as long as you can. Absorb the meaning of what you see—visitor centers and park rangers make this interpretation utterly painless and vastly interesting. You will never forget your visit if you take full advantage of it.

The rangers are carefully selected, highly skilled men. They see to it that you don't unconsciously abuse these areas which belong to you. They answer ten thousand questions a day with patient good humor. They will arrest you for speeding and risk their lives to rescue you if you get in trouble climbing a mountain. They will identify a rare wildflower for a group of school children, then go off to trap a grizzly bear and cart him off to a remote section where he won't annoy the visitors. They will also patch up the people who insist on feeding bears despite thousands of warnings against it. Rangers are to be treated with respect.

Once this book goes to press, parks may become inadequate at the squiggle of a Presidential pen. Cape Cod has just become part of the National Park System and new areas seem slated to join it: a patch of the Ozarks in Missouri, a piece of prairie in Kansas, the southern Indiana farmlands where Lincoln grew up, and other spots in other states. The ways of Congress are too imponderable to guess what will soon be included in this public pleasuring ground. But you may rest assured that the newest addition will be just as rewarding to visit as the parks and monuments that you will meet in these pages.

Camping Information

Though national park areas are free, or nearly so, touring them can be expensive. A family of four can spend $30-50 a day for meals, gas, accommodations, and incidentals. If this stretches your budget, consider camping, even if you are a complete novice. Families of modest means travel from coast to coast and back—camping at night, cooking their own meals—and scarcely spend more than if they had stayed home.

Here is the condensed advice of canvas and campstove veterans. First, plan ahead. Know where you will camp each night. The nation's camping facilities are listed in several directories (see below). Try to arrive by 5:00 P.M., local time. Popular camping areas fill up early; also by arriving well before dark you'll have plenty of time to set up camp, fix supper, and relax a bit before the campfire talk.

Everyone, even small children, should be assigned specific chores. This speeds up making and breaking camp, preparing meals, doing the beds and dishes, and improves morale all around.

Don't overequip. An umbrella tent, a sleeping bag apiece, and air mattresses (at least for adults) is enough for the sleeping department. Don't skimp when buying sleeping bags. Get good warm ones. Down-filled are best and pack smallest, although the price might make you blanch. But they are not essential. In any event, be sure to read the label listing the filling material. Avoid anything containing cotton. A good bag has a puffy feel. On warm nights you can sleep on top of the bag, but when it gets cold—and forty is not unusual in the mountains—you'll be glad you spent the extra money.

Check all tent types before buying. You may prefer a "pop tent" that goes up fast, or one with aluminum frame outside.

You may think of using cots—"they're more like beds at home." Don't do it; one folded cot is as bulky as a tent, and the chill comes up through to you from below. Get good, rubberized-cloth air mattresses that inflate by mouth through a valveless plug. Do not overinflate; the heaviest part of the body should sink almost to the ground; otherwise you'll roll around all night like an egg on a table.

For cooking, nesting aluminum sets are fine, but for eating, most campers prefer nonheat-conducting plastic. Paper plates and cups save a lot of dishwashing. Write names on cups and reuse them until you move on.

Cook with wood when you can (that's real camping), but for rainy days or late arrivals take along a two-burner gasoline (or canned-gas) stove. Pack a hatchet, camp shovel, insect bomb, large water jug, tarpaulin, lots of clothesline, and assorted plastic bags. Take a duffel bag for each person. The man of the tent should carry a sheath knife. Don't forget can opener, spatula, pot holders (or gardening gloves), scouring pads, detergent, aluminum foil, paper towels, shish-kebab skewers, and about 5,000 book matches carried in a plastic bag.

Flashlights and lantern are musts, but well-ordered camps don't need much artificial light. Ice chests are often more bother than help—except at "permanent" camps, where you may stay a week. Use canned, packaged, and instant foods. Buy your fresh meat and fruits when it is convenient and eat it soon.

You'll want a car-top luggage carrier, even if you have a station wagon. Preferably, make or order a lightweight, waterproof wooden or metal box designed to fit. Suction cups and drain-ledge clasps hold it securely and you'll soon forget it's there. Use the box as an attic; stow things you won't need during the day—camping gear, cold-weather clothing, extra shoes. Each side of the box should be hinged, allowing you to stand beside the car and reach in. A center partition helps keep things in place.

A small utility trailer simplifies everything and, if evenly loaded, actually takes weight off the car. If you want to be really elegant, investigate a camping trailer. They come with built-in double bunks that pull out from the sides, like drawers, and an integral tent that flips up and fastens all around. Not much room for living, but quick, comfortable, and efficient. It tows beautifully, as fast as you want to go, and can be parked with all your belongings. And if you are caught in a night rain, it dries faster and neater than a tent.

Carry food and eating equipment in the car or trunk for lunches and for replenishing as you pass grocery stores and wayside markets. Keep food and utensils separate. Two wooden boxes, marked "kitchen" and "pantry," with hinged lids, simplify everything; 12 by 12 by 24 inches is big enough. Simple hooks secure the contents from night-foraging animals.

A large pot with a fitting wire basket (or an old-fashioned wash boiler) is great for storing pots and dishes. Fill it with water and put it to heat early. After dinner, throw in everything you have used, slosh the basket up and down and then lift it out to rinse and drain the utensils.

Where to camp: All national parks, many national monuments, all national forests, most state parks, and private camps. For listings, with directions for getting there and the kind of facilities you will find: *Campground Guide for Tent and Trailer Tourists,* Campgrounds Unlimited, Blue Rapids, Kansas ($1.00); and *Campground Directory,* American Automobile Association (for members only). Also see *Camping Facilities,* and *State Parks, Areas, Acreages, and Accommodations,* National Park Service, Washington 25, D.C. You may write the State Park Director in the various state capitals; National Campers and Hikers Association, National Newark Building, Newark 2, New Jersey; or such local outdoor organizations as California's Sierra Club and Washington D.C.'s Potomac Appalachian Trail Club.

Aluminum-frame tent needs no stakes, can easily be carried even while set up.

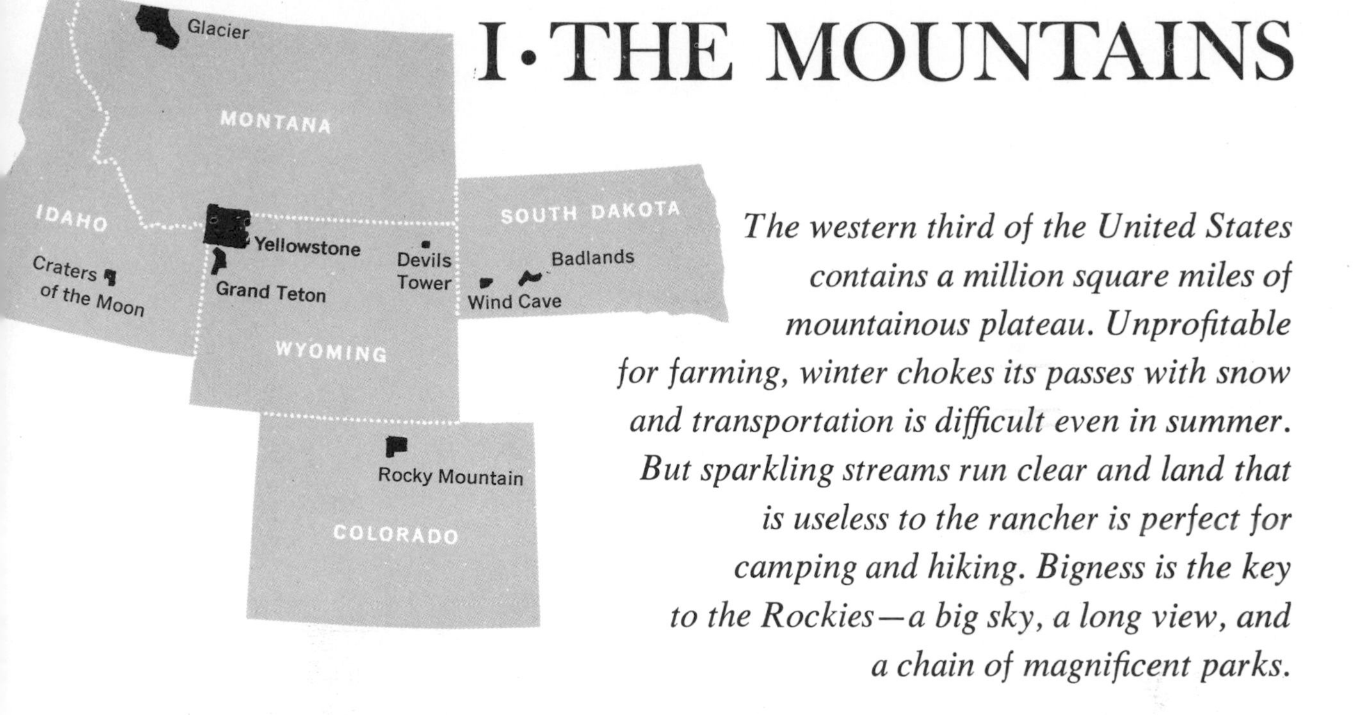

I·THE MOUNTAINS

The western third of the United States contains a million square miles of mountainous plateau. Unprofitable for farming, winter chokes its passes with snow and transportation is difficult even in summer. But sparkling streams run clear and land that is useless to the rancher is perfect for camping and hiking. Bigness is the key to the Rockies—a big sky, a long view, and a chain of magnificent parks.

Yellowstone National Park WYOMING

In August, 1877, a party of tourists camped near a spot in the northwestern corner of Wyoming, now called Madison Junction. Among them were Mr. George Cowan and his wife, Ida, who had come on horseback to see if the wild stories they had heard about the world's first national park were true.

Suddenly a small band of Indians appeared, scouts for a larger party of Nez Percé Indians with their families and belongings. They were in retreat from the U.S. Army, after misunderstandings in Idaho. Following a short powwow, the Indians took the group of tourists as hostages and continued their flight. Later, a couple of the white men panicked and in the scramble that followed, Mr. Cowan was shot in the thigh and head and left to die where he lay. Mrs. Cowan and the others were soon released unharmed.

Cowan was tough, and dragged himself in great pain for three days back to camp. He lived long to tell his remarkable tale.

The Lower Falls of the Yellowstone River plunge 309 feet downward into the head of Yellowstone Canyon.

Today, travel in Yellowstone is easier and safer. Good highways lead to five separate entranceways, and within the park, about 300 miles of paved road lead past most places of interest. Few Indians live in the area and the last ones seen in the park were tourists themselves.

Yellowstone has no caves, surf, or glaciers, but it has practically every other kind of display nature has to offer. Geysers shoot tons of water hundreds of feet into the air. Boiling pools, steam jets, mud volcanoes, and hot springs litter the landscape. There is a huge cliff of black glass, a great lake of unusual beauty, and a pond with two outlets, one leading to the Mississippi River and the other to the Pacific Ocean. There are rugged mountains, rolling meadows, and an endless forest of pines. Wild animals by the thousand roam at will without fear of man. Petrified trees stand erect. Stupendous waterfalls pour into a thousand-foot-deep canyon of blazing yellow rock.

No other area on earth has such a concentration of nature's spectacles. And all result, one way or another, from Yellowstone's unique volcanic origins.

Once there was a great valley here. But the

Old Faithful jets 15,000 gallons of hot water hourly.

crust of the earth was weak, and rifts crossed the area. From time to time, as the earth's crust shifted, the cracks opened and smoking rivers of lava spewed forth and filled the valley with molten rock. Clouds of volcanic ash shot into the air and fell back to earth, smothering all living things. As the ages went by the surface layers cooled and forests grew again; but the heat of those primeval eruptions remains below, and continues to supply power for the amazing natural displays that go on all the time in Yellowstone National Park.

Most famous of these, perhaps, are the geysers. Almost everyone has seen pictures of Old Faithful, a great white plume standing majestically on a domed expanse, with tourists clustering nearby, and Old Faithful Inn standing behind. No natural object in America, with the possible exception of Niagara Falls, is so familiar through photographs. So a person who approaches it for the first time might feel just a little bit bored, as if he had seen it all before. As for those timed eruptions, he might think that there is some sort of theatrical fakery about them.

Yellowstone rangers tell about the young man who found an old piece of iron grating and put it on the barren rock in front of the boardwalk that passes Old Faithful. When he heard the thumps and rumblings that signal an eruption, he leaned over and shouted into the grating: "Let her go, Joe!" And sure enough, Old Faithful went into her act. It had been doing so, of course, about once an hour, day and night, winter and summer, ever since it was discovered by white men over a hundred years ago and probably for thousands of years before.

But what the tourist takes for granted here is actually a most unusual and amazing natural phenomenon. Only in three other places in the world are geysers found; New Zealand, Iceland, and Chile.

Here's what happens when Old Faithful spouts. Cold water from melted snows and occasional rains trickles through cracks and channels in the hard volcanic rock that underlies the geyser basins. It collects in natural chambers hundreds of feet below the surface. The rock at these levels is continuously heated by gases, mostly natural steam, rising from deep-lying molten rock. For a while, the cool water absorbs the heat, but soon it starts to boil. To the onlooker this is seen as a tossing of water in the three-foot-wide spout. Then quickly more of the trapped water vaporizes, forcing the spouting column higher. Then, with the weight of the overlying water lessened, great volumes in the hot chambers suddenly flash into steam, and Old Faithful's column rises grandly in higher and higher spurts. A hundred, a hundred and twenty-five, sometimes a hundred and seventy feet it climbs in a continuous pulsating jet. For four minutes its elegant dance continues, its head crowned by a rising plume of vapor. Then, energy expended, it slowly shrinks and grows quiet, to gather strength for an hour and erupt again.

Some of the magic of a theater lies in being a part of the audience that responds together to a performance. When the theater is empty the magic is gone. But nature, unlike a human actor, goes on and on with its inevitable rhythms whether there is a full house or not. To see Old Faithful while standing with a group of tourists is to see a magnificent sight. But walk out alone in the black hours of early morning. Sit quietly and wait. Then when the earth begins to throb and fifteen thousand gallons of steaming water roar into the endless quiet of the starry sky—then you may come to know something about the earth and its forces that will never leave you.

Old Faithful is only one of two hundred geysers at Yellowstone. They come in all sizes and shapes. Some squirt continuously. Some wait days between eruptions and then play for hours. Grand Geyser's interval is eight to forty hours, but when it goes off it is really something to see. It erupts in a series of explosive discharges that cast rocketing bursts of water 200 feet into the air.

Most geysers follow a line running roughly north from Old Faithful for about twenty miles. They lie in groups: Upper, Midway, Lower, Gibbon and Norris Geyser Basins. Norris is one grand steaming expanse of barren white ground. This stony surface, called *sinter,* has been deposited in thin layers by the geysers' cooling run-off water. In places these layers are hollow underneath. So boardwalks have been laid down to prevent people from breaking through. Those walks may not be very pretty, but they protect you from scalding your feet and they guard the natural features from damage.

Many of the park's features are neatly described by their names: Whirligig, Pinwheel, and Steamboat geysers; Black Growler Steam Vent, Splutter Pot, Palpitator Spring. And at Norris, for those who are interested, there are some unnatural but welcome sights: Parking Area, Museum, and Comfort Station.

Even visitors who spend their full 30-day limit at a campground won't have time to see all of Yellowstone. Rather than speeding through, glancing at everything, try stopping at any spot that takes your fancy. Study it awhile. And if you

Grand Prismatic Spring spills hot water over its rim, where the nearby vegetation is smothered by mineral deposits.

Obsidian Cliff is a huge outcropping of natural black volcanic glass. Its shiny face is coated with lichens.

see a lesser path going off somewhere, follow it. The most humble little geyser or boiling spring is awe-inspiring when stumbled on unexpectedly and alone.

Yellowstone attracts crowds. But people collect at the obvious places. Those who enjoy company will be comfortable. And those who enjoy solitude and discovery can find it without trouble. A five-minute walk along an offshoot path will bring you to a silent wilderness. But *stay on the trails*. Yellowstone is big—about half as big as Massachusetts. Getting lost in it is no trick at all. If it happens to you, or if you sprain an ankle, hold still and holler. Smart hikers take along a whistle. It carries farther than a shout, and is less tiring. As a last resort, follow the streams downhill. Remember, Yellowstone lies in a huge basin, and its roads run close by its rivers.

In general, Yellowstone is safer than any city. Its animals leave you alone if you don't molest them. Its altitude is too high for poisonous snakes. Nature here is vast and lonely, but it is not belligerent.

To the right of the Loop Road, going north from Norris, lies Roaring Mountain. Dozens of steam vents pierce its ashen sides. These are fumaroles, outlets for magmatic steam—the same steam that heats the rocks of the geyser basins. Roaring Mountain gots its name from the noise made by steam blasting out of a small orifice that broke through in 1902. Soon the hole opened up enough to reduce the noise, but the total volume of escaping gases remains undiminished.

Farther along stands Obsidian Cliff—the mountain of glass mentioned by Jim Bridger, one of the West's most famous mountain men. Jim was a huge, wiry man, born in Richmond, Virginia, in 1804. He soon felt the lure of the western mountains and by the middle of the 19th century there wasn't a beaver stream in the Rockies he hadn't explored. He early decided that, when telling anecdotes, a man who stuck to fact simply didn't have any imagination. Here's how his story comes down to us:

"I camp yonder in a meadow, and went lookin' for meat. Soon I see an elk a right spell yonder.

The long-eared mule deer is common in the west.

A bull moose noses underwater for succulent algae.

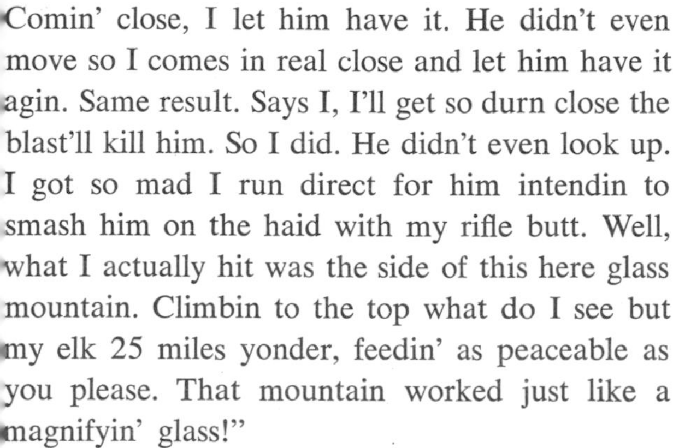

Comin' close, I let him have it. He didn't even move so I comes in real close and let him have it agin. Same result. Says I, I'll get so durn close the blast'll kill him. So I did. He didn't even look up. I got so mad I run direct for him intendin to smash him on the haid with my rifle butt. Well, what I actually hit was the side of this here glass mountain. Climbin to the top what do I see but my elk 25 miles yonder, feedin' as peaceable as you please. That mountain worked just like a magnifyin' glass!"

Like all Jim Bridger's stories, this one contains a basis of truth. Obsidian Cliff is not exactly a mountain, but it certainly is made of glass—pure volcanic glass. Its chemical composition is the same as that of a coke bottle. But it is not transparent. The glass itself is a smoky black, and the broken face of the cliff is rough and covered with lichens.

Obsidian Cliff was once a kind of arsenal for the Indians from miles around. Here they came to make arrow and spear heads and skinning knives from the even-textured and easily split glass boulders. A nearby field exhibit explains the geologic and human history of the cliff.

Today, as in Jim Bridger's time, the elk feed as peaceably as you please, for Yellowstone is the greatest wildlife refuge in the world outside Africa. The elk come each summer—ten thousand of them—to munch the lush grasses of the high meadows. The bull elk is a majestic animal, averaging 700 pounds, with his flowing dark mane and widespread antlers.

Wolves have long since been eliminated from the western United States and now the elk tend to multiply beyond the ability of their range to support them. So limited hunting is allowed outside the park each fall, as the elk leave for their winter feeding grounds in the lowlands.

Mule deer and moose also abound, but not in large herds. The moose particularly is a solitary beast. He likes to graze on underwater plants in the shallows of lakes and streams. It is fine indeed to come on a moose, head plunged into the water

Elk graze on Gibbon Meadow and move up to Jackson Hole in the fall. A bull may top 1,000 pounds.

Elusive dwellers of the high mountains, bighorn rams charge head-on with echoing crashes during mating duels.

and huge palmated antlers waving just above the surface, and then see him raise up suddenly with plants hanging from his mouth and water cascading off his great bony head.

With the exception of the wolf, all other wild animals native to the area still flourish. There are mule deer and marmots, beaver and bighorn sheep, bison and pronghorn. Park officials are particularly proud of the bison herd. In the early days the park staff was too small to protect such a large area from poachers. By 1900 only 30 buffalo remained in the park. Now the Yellowstone herd has grown to about 500 animals, about normal for the area, and that's the way the Park Service intends to keep it. The herds live mostly in the remote eastern section, accessible only by trail.

Bison, once numerous in America, have been saved from extinction. About 500 live in Yellowstone Park.

Ten miles beyond Obsidian Cliff, going north on the Loop Road, lies Mammoth Hot Springs, an area with a split personality. Mammoth is both a thermal spectacle and a village. Does your car need repairs? At Mammoth Village there is a garage. Not feeling well? A hospital with complete medical, surgical, and ambulance service is nearby. Need supplies? The general store sells nearly everything. Mammoth also contains a post office, hotel, cabins, campground, restaurant, and chapel which holds services for most religious denominations. All these facilities are operated privately.

Park headquarters is also here. A visitor center explains the features of the area. Naturalists conduct free evening programs in an amphitheater.

Grizzly bears, normally shy, feast at a garbage dump.

Fleet pronghorns appear in the park's northern areas.

The hot springs themselves flow from a hillside nearby. They don't spout or erupt or squirt, they simply run steadily. But what they lack in spectacle they make up in beauty.

The hard sinter pans of the geyser basins build up slowly, perhaps a thirty-second of an inch a year. But hot spring terraces are made of calcium carbonate–limestone–and they form at a rate of up to a foot a year.

Here is how a hot spring works: rain water and snow melt picks up carbonic gas from vegetation on the surface, and then seeps into the ground. The mountains in this area are limestone–sediments formed at the bottom of ancient seas, then uplifted. Water containing carbonic gas is a powerful solvent for the limey rock. Heated by volcanic fires it attacks the rock rapidly, carving great hidden caverns deep within the mountains. Eventually the water emerges from cracks and as it meets the air it begins to cool and the gases are driven out.

Now the dissolved limestone will no longer stay

Otter families play beside Yellowstone's clear streams.

Trumpeter swans honk shrilly from secluded lakes.

Terraces of travertine at Mammoth Hot Springs build up quickly from the overflow of limey hot water.

in solution and it deposits at the lip of the spring. Gradually the lip grows. Then, rising tier on tier, great terraces form. Certain species of algae find a home in these steaming waters and add color to the lovely forms. Yellows and orange on the lower levels complement the snowy white of the limestone where the water runs hottest.

Morning Glory Pool owes its name to algae that fringe it. Tiny plants change hue as the run-off water cools.

The amount of stone that hot springs can deposit is amazing. Enormous mounds and shelves build up. A short distance from the springs lie the Hoodoos, a profusion of stone blocks as big as houses. They originally stood as a broad shelf at the mouth of a spring high on a mountainside. It got so big it simply broke away and came crashing into the valley in chunks.

This form of deposited limestone is called travertine. There are whole hills of it in Italy and Greece. The ancients loved to build temples of travertine, for it is easy to carve and lovely in texture.

At Tower Junction, 18 miles east of Mammoth, the Loop Road meets the Northeast Entrance Road, and the Lamar River joins the Yellowstone. The Lamar Valley with its surrounding mountains is a lovely wilderness area. Here you can walk for hours, even days, and never see another person. And on the south rim of the valley, high on the face of the cliffs, stand petrified trees. They were buried for millions of years by volcanic outpourings, but erosion is now disclosing huge examples of petrifaction—whole trunks, up to six feet in diameter and ten feet high, standing erect with stony roots still gripping the soil. In all, scientists have counted 27 layers of petrified forests. Each took root in a rich layer of volcanic ash. Each in turn was smothered by a new eruption.

Jim Bridger claimed he knew a spot in Yellowstone Canyon that had a delayed-action echo. After bedding down for the night he would raise his head from his saddle and holler, "Wake up, Jim!" then go to sleep. Along about dawn the echo would come back from the distant canyon walls and rouse him.

No one has heard that echo since, but Yellowstone is full of strange sounds. Coyotes sing at night. Bears knock trash cans about. Geysers hiss and roar. Steam jets whistle. Wind soughs in the pines. Mud volcanoes thump and pop. Birds by the thousand sing and scold. Streams gurgle and cleave the air with the continuous thunder of their waterfalls.

Perhaps the strangest noise in the park is the rarest. It is possible that such a sound has been heard at no other place. Here is a report written in 1924 by Jack Haynes, who spent his life in Yellowstone.

Black bears are a common sight near roads and campgrounds. They may appear tame, but are unpredictable.

"Our small boat was approaching Pelican Roost Island. The lake was mirror-like in the stillness of early morning. A sound rose overhead apparently

Pelicans roost at Pelican Island in Yellowstone Lake. The park is host to some 200 species of birds.

Lower Falls of the Yellowstone, here seen from below on Uncle Tom's Trail, are twice as high as Niagara.

from the west beginning with a low roar which gradually became louder and rose in pitch, then gradually faded away. . . . Then from another direction a similar sound was heard and again from still another direction. . . . It was a mystifying sound which none of us in the boat was able to explain. . . . It is easy to imagine that we heard the sound effect that would have been used in a stage reproduction of the spectacle of an aurora borealis."

Yellowstone Lake lies at an altitude of 7,731 feet. The sound probably was connected with a static electrical charge accumulating in the rarified air over the great body of water. This is borne out by the fact that in 1885 a man who was sitting next to the mast of a small sailboat was killed by a bolt of lightning, though there was not a cloud in the sky.

Today sailboats are not allowed on the lake, but not because of the danger from lightning; the tragic event of 1885 was a unique incident. The danger lies in the simple fact that Yellowstone Lake is huge. It is 20 miles long and 14 miles wide, and storms come up quickly in the Rockies. In a few minutes the normally placid surface can be whipped into a nasty, choppy sea. You can rent a boat for fishing or just sightseeing, if you wish, or you can launch your own boat from a trailer, but a smart boatman checks the weather first.

The outlet of Yellowstone Lake forms the Yellowstone River—for 15 miles it meanders, clear and swift-running, through a lovely country of forest and meadow. Then it gathers strength and rushes for a magnificent double plunge into a world of craggy beauty.

It gathers speed as it passes under the Chittenden Bridge, tucking up its skirts as if it knows what is to come, for it is headed for two magnificent, thundering leaps. You can take a side road and see the Lower Falls from a distance at Artist Point. But a better way is to park by the Chittenden Bridge and walk across it. On your left, the South Rim Trail takes off, following the bank of the river. Walk along it through the pines. The river rushes faster and faster alongside. Then suddenly in a great green arc it charges over the Upper Falls, dropping 109 feet into a churning white basin.

Again the white water collects itself and races along the now-deepening gorge. Then, in an almost leisurely fashion, it approaches the lip of Lower Falls. Here a great mass of hard volcanic rock stands like a great dam. Through thousands of years, slowly and with almost surgical precision, the endless waters have cut a notch. The river is literally squeezed together at this point and shot into space, as if poured from a pitcher—60,000 gallons a second during spring run-off. Three hundred and nine feet it plunges, green at the lip and turning white as it drops in a continuous trunk of spray. And as it falls clear and free down the vertical face of the cliff it carries with it a hurricane of air which explodes from its foot in a blast of roaring mist.

This is the beginning of the Grand Canyon of the Yellowstone, a noble slash in the old earth's crust. Here again the volcanic past of Yellowstone is evident. The canyon walls are made up of many outpourings of lava. This cooked rock, ryolite, is yellow by nature. Weathering has streaked its pinnacles and spires with black.

Until a few years ago you could walk to the bottom, down a series of wooden steps fastened to the canyon face, and along a path by the edge of the rapids. Uncle Tom's Trail, they called it. It wasn't an easy walk. Spray from the falls drenches the trail. But at the end an eerie sight awaited: by the very edge of the foaming river, and seeming oddly out of place at the bottom of those towering yellow walks, the throat of a geyser sputters and steams. Uncle Tom's Trail is now closed, although the Park Service is now working on plans to have it reopened. Formerly, the Park Service had thought that the sight of people at the bottom of the canyon detracted from the view of those above. No date has been set for its reopening, so check with Park Headquarters before setting out to see this remarkable trail.

Yellowstone National Park

NW corner of Wyoming. Area: 3,472 sq. mi.

Season: May 1-Oct. 1, facilities June 1-Sept. 25.

Climate: warm days, cool nights; elev. 7,500 ft.

Accommodations: hotels, lodges, cabins, trailer park.

Services: restaurants, garages, car rental, hospital, chapel, service in park.

Trains and buses are met by park buses.

Moose graze in a wild meadow beside the Yellowstone River. Open country patches the quilt of dense forest.

Grand Teton National Park WYOMING

Most mountains are surrounded by foothills, and sometimes it is hard to tell where the hills stop and the mountains begin. But in Grand Teton National Park you can walk across a meadow, put out your hand and lean on them—almost. Nowhere else do such superb peaks rise so abruptly from the flat.

The Teton Range is not the highest in the Rockies, nor is Jackson Hole the greenest and lushest valley. It is the combination of the two that is matchless. Also there is a special quality about the mountains themselves—the crystalline hardness of the rocks, the way the peaks rise in glinting spires, the awesome canyons that cut between them. And no other valley can boast a finer river than the Snake, rushing clear and smooth over its firm bed of cobbles and sand. Where the valley meets the mountains a string of lakes lies sparkling: Jackson, Leigh, Jenny, Bradley, Taggart and Phelps, each ringed on one side by a silent forest of pines and on the other by the wall of the Tetons themselves.

Grand Teton National Park consists of a 30-mile section of the Teton Range, along with most of Jackson Hole (trappers of the 1820's and 30's called any valley ringed by mountains a "hole." This one was named for David E. Jackson). In all, the park's area is about 500 square miles. Most visitors content themselves simply with looking at the Tetons from the road in their car, or from a boat on Jackson or Jenny Lake. Others take saddle trips from the corrals at Jackson Lake Lodge or Jenny Lake. In any case few of them get into the mountains themselves.

Only those who get out and walk up into the canyons will really know how magnificent this range is. Perhaps the best introduction to Grand Teton's 175 miles of trails is the one that goes up Cascade Canyon. You can get to it by walking a couple of miles around Jenny Lake, or you can ferry over in a motor boat to a landing near the mouth of the canyon. From there a switchback

trail leads to a spot with the uninspired name of "Inspiration Point," which affords a view of the Hole that is fine indeed.

Beyond, stretching three and a half miles due west, lies Cascade Canyon. The walk is well worth it. The trail skirts beaver ponds, crosses meadows spangled with wildflowers, passes beneath great boulder slides where whistling marmots and squeaking pikas live. You may see a Shiras moose, or a mule deer, or a black bear—the shy, not the begging kind—and towering unbelievably overhead stand the sheer rock faces, the hanging cliffs, the blue-gray towers of the Tetons. From the valley they present a lovely profile against the sky. Here in the canyon they show in all their im-

Jackson Lake sprawls at the base of the steeply rising Teton Range. This view is from Signal Mountain.

mensity, crowding the canyon floor like the walls of a colossal corridor. They soar a full mile overhead, hung with remnant glaciers and streaming with foaming snow-melt.

Beyond, to the left, stands the Grand Teton itself, 13,766 feet high, an impressive sight to the eye and a challenge to climbers.

Mountain climbing is a new and fast-growing sport in the United States. In a civilization that seems to have too many escalators, power mowers, electric can openers, and automatic gadgets of all kinds, there is something direct and satisfying about clambering up the raw and solid surface of a mountain simply to get to the top.

Experienced climbers rate the Tetons among the finest climbing mountains in the world. There is variety to suit every degree of skill, from novice to expert. The rock is solid, non-crumbling granite, and the weather is just about perfect. The Grand itself is very much like Switzerland's Matterhorn. Profiles of the two are similar, and the actual climb—7,000 vertical feet—is equal.

Unique in the United States is the Exum Mountain Climbing School at Jenny Lake. You don't have to know anything about climbing to attend the classes. Simply drop in and sign up for the kind of mountaineering you want. Beginners are

Riders pause at Jenny Lake Lodge. Horses can be hired nearby at Jackson Lake for pack trips or picnics.

taught fundamentals of rope work and rock scaling. Experts can brush up on technical climbing with pitons, caribiners and the like. One day will prepare you for the lesser climbs, and if you show aptitude, you can join a group and scale the Grand itself, a two-day effort with stop-over at a camp 11,500 feet up. Solo climbing is not permitted, and all climbers must register at the Jenny Lake Ranger Station before starting.

"Anyone with a sturdy body and desire can climb," says Exum. His parties include twelve-year-olds as well as those in their sixties.

It is not surprising that the Tetons seem to rise right from the floor of Jackson Hole, because geologically speaking that is exactly what they did. About a million years ago there were no mountains here. Beds of sandstone and limestone 3,000 feet thick covered the granite base rocks. Then a great crack, or fault, appeared, running north and south. The land to the east of the fault sank and to the west it rose—not all at once, but in stages. Whenever the forces deep within the earth overcame the friction of the fault faces the rock lurched a few feet. When this sort of thing happens today we call it an earthquake.

All in all, the vertical displacement along the Teton fault exceeded 20,000 feet. But in early Ice Ages, erosion chipped away at the mountains, and the ground-up pieces washed into the valley. Then about 10,000 years ago, in the last Ice Age, colossal glaciers smothered the gorges and speeded up the sculpturing process. Today only about 7,000 feet of the face of the fault is visible in the toothy skyline. All the old sedimentary layers have been ground away—all but those that covered Mount Moran, where a flat cap remains. The great glaciers have long since melted, but the work they did produced Jackson Hole and the Tetons as we see them today—the canyons, the peaks, the lovely lakes strung at their bases. Each lake is the scooped-out basin where the great trunk glaciers once buried their snouts.

The floor of Jackson Hole is made up of assorted gravel and rock too porous to hold water, and much of the valley is covered by sage brush, a native of much drier areas. Here and there great bowl-like depressions pock the ground. Huge blocks of ice sometimes were left buried in the gravel when the glaciers receded. When they eventually melted the earth collapsed behind them, leaving the so-called "pot-holes."

There are other things to do in the park besides

Elk from Yellowstone winter at Jackson Hole refuge.

hike, climb, or ride. The lakes and the Snake River offer excellent trout fishing. You can rent boats on Jenny or Jackson Lakes, or you can launch your own from a trailer at Colter Bay. You can join a moonlight cruise on Jackson Lake, with a picnic on an island. You can take an all-day float trip down the Snake on a rubber raft. Make reservations at Jackson Lake Lodge. Campfire programs are held nightly.

Accommodations will fit any purse. Jenny Lake Lodge and Jackson Lake Lodge are luxurious and expensive. Make reservations early from Grand Teton Lodge Company, Moran, Wyoming. Private dude ranches are scattered throughout the valley. Write Grand Teton National Park, Moose, Wyoming for a list. There are cabins at Colter Bay, and a modern trailer camp set among the trees. Also at Colter Bay is one of the finest campgrounds to be found anywhere. Nearby are modern stores, restaurants, laundry and public showers.

Frontier Airlines provides daily service from Salt Lake City to an airport right in the park. There is no rail service, but buses meet the Union Pacific at Victor, Idaho.

But most people come by car. The roads to and within the park are excellent. Check a Wyoming road map. No matter how you come, your first stop should be the new visitor center at Moose. There you will find a very fine exhibit telling the fascinating history of the region.

Grand Teton National Park

NW Wyoming, near Jackson. Area: 484 sq. mi.
Season: June 15-Labor Day; road open all year.
Climate: warm days, cool nights; elev. 6,500 ft.
Accommodations: lodges, cabins, trailer grounds.
Services: stores, garages, car rental, hospital, service in park.
Major highways including US 26, 287, and 189 lead to park.

Huge rubber rafts take parties of 18 daily on float trips on the Snake River from Buffalo Fork to Moose.

Glacier National Park MONTANA

This great preserve displays nature's splendors on a majestic scale. Many regard this as the most beautiful and impressive of all our national parks. Named for the prehistoric glaciers that carved its scenery, it shows what earth-shaking changes natural forces can bring about. Even today 60-odd glaciers long past their prime still cling to these mountains.

One awe-struck naturalist is quoted as having said of it, "This is where God stood when he created the world." Perhaps so. What we do know of its origins indicates an ages-long struggle between the up-thrust of the earth's crust that created the Rockies and the opposing forces of the great ice ages. The result is 1,500-plus square miles of high mountains, where more than 1,000 waterfalls pour down into streams that feed 200 lakes; where some glaciers have stabilized themselves in the last decade or so, because winters have been growing colder in northwest Montana, along the U.S.-Canadian border.

The park sprawls over into Canada. An additional 200 square miles is maintained as a park by the Canadian government—and the whole of it is officially named Waterton-Glacier International Peace Park, dedicated in ceremonies held in 1932. Inside the park you may cross the border with only a pause at customs.

Glacier's mountains, among the most rugged in the continent, rise abruptly out of the prairie like a windowless wall. And to early explorers and Pacific-bound pioneers that's just what they were —a nearly impassable barrier.

Its peaks began to rise out of the earth's crust, along with the rest of the Rockies, about 60 million years ago. But while the rest of the Rockies grew straight and orderly, this region was gripped by vise-like pressures which caused it to buckle and squeeze together. The crust, carrying the newborn mountains with it, was forced sideways into a gigantic fold, like a loose rug that has been scuffed. The folded earth finally broke under the strain, and then, as the pressure continued, an immense amount of the stuff of earth was shoved eastward over the flat Montana plain. The mountains that now make up Glacier's east wall were moved about 18 miles. It was, as is evident in the mangled geological formations, a rough ride.

Today, these mountains are known as the Lewis Range, in honor of Meriwether Lewis of the Lewis

Upper St. Mary's Lake, at eastern border of park, shows mountain slopes sculptured by ancient glaciers.

Rocky Mountain goat, nimble climber of wild heights, has splayed hooves with soft center pads to grip rocks.

and Clark expedition, who came upon it in 1804. The remains of the cataclysm causing such rugged rockiness has been named the Lewis Overthrust by geologists, who come from all over the world to study it.

If the range had stayed as the overthrust left it, about the only way it could be viewed today would be from an airplane. Its immense shambles would even have stopped the Rocky Mountain goats that now scramble over it. But the Ice Age

came and brought the great earth-shapers that gave the park its beauty—and its name: the glaciers.

The first big glaciers formed about 160,000 years ago when the Ice Age gripped many northern regions of the world. First there were snowdrifts. As the drifts got deeper, the weight of each new snowfall built up pressure on the lower layers, eventually turning them into granular snow and finally into solid ice.

Below a depth of 100 feet, all ice becomes "plastic"—in effect a very thick fluid. Thus when glaciers reach a certain size they begin to flow, to advance. As they flow these great rivers of ice pick up rocks, which become their working tools. Huge boulders, tiny pebbles, all are carried along like the teeth of a giant file. They are enough to slice mountains, cut the sides and floors of valleys, gouge out the deep basins that later become lakes.

At the height of the Ice Age, the valleys of the park were completely filled with glaciers up to 3,000 feet thick. They covered all but the highest peaks and overflowed far beyond the mountains. The great glacier which filled Two Medicine Valley, at the park's east entrance, extended for 40 miles onto the Montana plain.

After many thousands of years, the climate turned warm again. The glaciers melted. Then the Ice Age came back in full force, and the cycle was repeated. The last Ice Age ended about 12,000 years ago. Since then there have been several periods of cold, but of less drastic extent.

Since the beginning of this century all the glaciers have been shrinking, and dozens have disappeared. The biggest one left is Sperry, high above the Avalanche Campground in the McDonald Valley region. In 1900, it covered 840 acres and the ice along its front edge was well over 500 feet thick. Now it covers fewer than 300 acres and its ice front is a mere 100 feet thick. However, the warming period which brought this about, beginning in 1900, seems to have reversed itself since the late '40's. Colder winters have stabilized the dwindling glacier. Otherwise it would have been gone by now.

Glacier Park does not have a corner on the

A ranger-naturalist leads a party of hikers across the face of Grinnell Glacier on one of the park's 1,000 miles of maintained trails. Trips on foot vary from two-hour walks to overnight expeditions.

Many Glacier Hotel, beside Lake Sherburne, is one of four hotels in the park, open during the summer.

nation's supply of glaciers. Elsewhere in Montana, Wyoming, Colorado, Washington, Oregon, and California there are a total of about 300 big glaciers. The biggest are far away on Mt. Rainier. Yet Glacier fully lives up to its name, for no other region on the continent tells the story of glacial ages so well.

This is the only region below the Canadian border with a sub-Arctic climate—like that of mid-Alaska. Plant and animal life of the park reflect this climate. During the short summer, highland meadows are rich with alpine blooms. Glacier lilies seem to warm the earth with their sun-like yellow. Blue gentians offer contrast. Red monkey flowers get into the act among yellow arnica. More than 100 different plants flower on the mountain meadows. Heavy forests add to the scenery, and they will look different to you if you come from the East. For the trees of Glacier Park, like those of all the western mountains, are practically all evergreen—chiefly pines, firs, spruces, hemlock and red cedar.

Many animals live here: moose, deer, bear, coyote, wolf, bighorn sheep, mountain goat, cougar, and fisher can all be seen.

Most celebrated of these are the Rocky Mountain goats, the aloof, almost mystic denizens of the highest peaks and the official animal of Glacier Park. They exist in most of the western mountain regions, but they are seldom seen except for the group of about 800 that lives in Glacier. Actually not a goat but a mountain antelope, kin to the chamois of the Alps, it is marvelously equipped for ice heights, having knife-sharp hoofs with soft center pads—virtual suction cups, able to cling to the slickest rock. And it has two coats of hair, like arctic animals, weatherproofing it against the worst that winter can do.

The Blackfeet Indian reservation adjoins Glacier Park.

Glacier was once the domain of the Blackfeet Indians. The government paid them $1,500,000 for their interests in the area. They now live on a very large reservation just to the east of Glacier. They often gather around the eastern entrance to the park, occasionally garbed in the great feathered head-dress of western Indians, and they sometimes greet you at Glacier Park Lodge. The Great Northern Railway is the only railroad to serve the Park, now.

Glacier's founders set out to guard the areas in all its natural beauty. The National Park Service, overseeing it as a recreation area has managed to handle an enormous tourist traffic efficiently. The park is open from about mid-June until mid-September. And during that time as many as 700,000 people visit it. But its wilderness remains undefiled in spite of more than 1,000 miles of trails and about 70 miles of roadway.

Chief tourist route is the Going-To-The-Sun Road, the only road to cross the park. As its name suggests, the road unfolds spectacular vistas. To savor the park's full meaning however, you should be prepared to take to some of its trails—which you must do to come upon its remaining glaciers. You may go by foot or by horseback on scheduled tours of a day or take longer and camp. Be sure you have proper clothing—Glacier Park is one of the most rugged pockets of wilderness left on the continent; casual raiment is entirely inadequate for a visit here.

Glacier may be reached from east or west by U.S. 93 or 89. Buses connect with Missoula, Shelby, and Great Falls, Montana. The Great Northern Railway stops at the park, with fine lodge facilities immediately at hand. The hotels are Glacier Park, Many Glacier, and Lake McDonald. Write to the Glacier Park, Inc. for reservations. Two chalets, Granite Park and Sperry, can be reached by trail. There are cabins available at Rising Sun and Many Glacier; and campgrounds are to be had at Sprague Creek, Rising Sun, Many Glacier, Two Medicine, and Apgar Village. There are also eight other remote campgrounds. Cafeterias are at the major centers, along with stores, garages and car rentals at East Glacier Park and Whitefish. Religious services are held at the various centers.

You may fish in the park without a license, but by rod in hand only. Bring your casting or spinning rod by all means; but be sure you are stocked with plugs—no live bait or flies are allowed.

You will find the heart of the park to be Waterton Lake, a large body of water which extends into both Canada and the U.S., with regular boat service crossing the boundary.

Glacier National Park is not the largest in the park system (though you could fit Rhode Island into it with much to spare). Its waterfalls are not the highest. It hasn't the most lakes. But what it does have is a marvelous balance of splendors.

There is the old saying about seeing Venice and then dying; but if you would be invigorated as you may seldom ever be, see Glacier and add years to your life.

Glacier National Park

NW Montana. Area: 1,583 sq. mi.

Season: June 15-Sept. 10.

Climate: brisk, occas. rain squalls; elev. 4,500 ft.

Accommodations: hotels, chalets, trailer and campgrounds.

Services: cafeterias, stores, garages, car rental, service in park.

Highways US 2, US 93, and US 89 lead to park.

Perpetual ice paves the floor of a shallow lava tube whose porous rock walls keep out the summer heat.

Craters of the Moon National Monument

IDAHO

Summers in southern Idaho are hot, for this is stark and dry country. The mountainous central plateau of the Rockies, it is broken only by the great plain of the Snake River where it curves north to meet the Columbia.

On the high northern flank of this plain lies Craters of the Moon National Monument, a 75-square-mile area which preserves some of the world's finest and most varied volcanic displays. The area derives its odd name from the resemblance, in miniature, of much of its terrain to a telescopic view of the surface of the moon.

There are many strange sights here—black lava flows tumbled like gigantic spills of fudge, blocks of lava big as a house, great desolate stretches of black jaggedness like acres and acres of spilled

ABOVE
Hardened lava of spatter cone has iridescent color.

RIGHT
Pahoehoe is slow-cooled lava that sets in ropy shapes.

coal, cinder cones and spatter cones looking like small replicas of their parent volcanoes.

What created the vast reaches of various lava was a series of fissures in the earth's surface that now extend consecutively for about 16 miles. Called the Great Rift, the fissures opened several times during ancient ages, spewing molten rock as hot as 2,000 Fahrenheit degrees for miles.

The last such flow is thought to have happened more than 1,650 years ago. But unlike lava deposits in wetter parts of the world, that in Craters of the Moon has not deteriorated because of the very low rainfall in this part of Idaho. This is another possible reason for its name, for it is also believed that the surface of the moon goes on in infinite sameness due to the lack of elements that would change or break down the components of its surface.

There are two kinds of lava, and their names are Hawaiian in origin: pahoehoe (pah-hoa-hoa) and aa (ah-ah)—meaning, first, a solidified lava which can be easily traveled upon, the second being broken slag, jagged and harsh to the feet. Craters of the Moon is plentifully supplied with both sorts.

The chief sights of the lava areas are the cinder cones and the spatter cones. Cinder cones were caused by sprayed lava-froth thrown high in the air, cooling in pebble-sized particles before falling. It piled as it fell, and one heap of it, 760 feet high, is believed to have resulted from fountain-like eruptions shooting up a thousand feet. The smaller spatter cones came from less violent outpours. Still molten as it fell, the sticky lava blobs formed jagged, steep-sided piles.

Another remarkable sight in Craters of the Moon National Monument is that of the underground caves or tubes. These were created when great streams of lava solidified on their outer surfaces, with the inner remaining molten until it drained away, leaving long passageways.

Where water has collected in these tubes over the centuries, seeping down from the meager rainfall of the area, it has been winter-frozen into streams and lakes of ice. And because of the fine insulation given by the porous lava shells of the tubes, the caves are cool and even very cold in the hottest of summer months. Sleds have even been used, although primarily for photographic purposes, during the hottest of outside weather.

And there are other worthy sights in the monument area. In winter, a sparse snow can occasionally make for memorable contrasts in black and white. And in flower-time, there are the expanses of dwarf wild buckwheat in clumps dotting slopes of the cinder cones, somehow finding reward for hungry roots in what will not be soil for ages to come. The bright orange leaves of bitterroot also put color among the cinders, doing it a second time when their white flower opens, blooming in dry heat. Another decoration is the monkey flower, which opens its face in yellow-spotted pink.

Preserved by the dry climate, spatter cones mark an ancient fault line where hot magma spouted and cooled.

Craters of the Moon is about 200 miles west from Yellowstone National Park. It is reached from either the town of Arco, 20 miles to the northeast on U.S. 20 and 26, or from Carey, 24 miles to the southwest on the same road. A visitor center just inside the entrance is close by a campground laid out in sparse bush. Loop Drive winds through the monument, and trails lead from marked points into the cave area and among the cones.

There are no great volcanic peaks here, such as Mount Rainier in Washington State, or Lassen in California. The lava poured out of the earth from great cracks or from the spatter and cinder cones in the Great Rift Zone. But that is the unique nature of Craters of the Moon National Monument, its contradictions: ice in the broiling summer, flowers appearing to grow from the lava, and caves without running water.

Craters of the Moon National Monument

S. Idaho. Area: 75 sq. mi.
Season: year round.
Climate: hot in summer, light snow in winter.
Accommodations: campground.
Services: visitor center.
Highways US 20 and US 26 lead to park.

Rocky Mountain National Park COLORADO

One of the great sights of America is the spectacle of the Rocky Mountains rising ahead as you travel west across the Great Plains. Shimmering beyond their blue foothills in the famous crystal-clear air of Colorado, they loom like a vast, white-topped wall. Coloradans call this the Front Range. It is the mightiest massing of mountains in all the continental United States. At its center is Rocky Mountain National Park, which holds no fewer than 65 peaks rising above 10,000 feet.

This grand gathering of mountains, now the goal, the highroad and the tenting grounds of vacationing Americans from all walks of life, has been 60 million years preparing. The geologists have fitted their bits of evidence together like a detective story, and decided that it was about that long ago that the whole Front Range thrust up out of the plains like a great long wrinkle in a carpet. Some wrinkle! It was 200 miles long and 40 miles across. Later, ice and water wore down the giant fold; now many peaks, even the tallest, Long's Peak (altitude 14,256 feet), have flat tops. Then came a period of renewed uplifting, and finally the Ice Ages. Everywhere you look you see the record left by the great glaciers. In fact, glaciation is what carved most of the scenery. The cliffs, the lakes, the enormous moraines. On a few high pockets there still remain a few slowly melting glaciers left behind from this period.

Of all the big parks in the West, Rocky Mountain National Park is the most popular, attracting 1,800,000 visitors a year. The park lies only 80 miles away from the big city of Denver, and within easy touring distance of the prairie states. It is the first spot that many travelers aim for on their way West. Its scenic splendors are what appeal and the park has been laid out so that all comers can see them. Rocky Mountain National Park is 406 square miles of unspoiled nature open to any hikers and horseback riders who want to try its 303 miles of back-country trails. It is also a vast tract of raw scenery traversed by

one superb highway. You can simply drive through the park, passing one unforgettable vist after another along the 49 miles of sky-touching highway between Estes Park Village at the eas entrance and Grand Lake at the Park's southwest corner, and be back in Denver by nightfall.

Whether you stop and camp in the park or not the trip over this highway is one you won't want

Long's Peak, the highest in Colorado, rises beyond Bear Lake. At 14,255 feet, it is a favorite for climbers.

to miss. Starting from Estes Park, a bustling town of shops, restaurants and motels, you head west on U.S. 34. In the first ten minutes past the Fall River entrance you may see deer or elk. Climbing, you arrive at Deer Ridge Junction, where Trail Ridge Road, the highway that will carry you right over the Rockies, properly begins. It is so named for the old Ute Indian trail that led over this very ridge. You can stop, look, and breathe the winy air at several viewing points along the way. At Many Parks Curve, the chipmunk, the ground squirrel, or Clark's nutcracker may take food from your hand. You look down across the eastern

An all-day climb to Long's Peak is strenuous but safe. All climbers must register at the ranger's station.

Rocky Mountain bighorn ewes graze on a high meadow. They are seen frequently on Specimen Mountain.

slope's many parks, or meadows. To the north is Fall River Valley, and behind it the peaks of the Mummy Range. To the south Long's Peak juts high beyond the flats of Beaver Meadows and Moraine Park. You can see several moraines below you—long, successive ridges of broken rocks built up at the edges of long-vanished glaciers and now thickly covered with forest.

Above Many Parks Curve, the highway climbs along the north side of Trail Ridge. To the right is Hidden Valley, much favored by skiers, for whom the road is kept open this far in winter. Beyond the two-mile elevation sign you find another parking area at Rainbow Curve. Here the Great Plains are in view far to the east, and close below, canyons thickly mantled in lodgepole pine.

At Rock Cut,one of the Park's most spectacular view points, you can see ice fields in the George Lakes area. Farther on you pass Iceberg Lake, fed by glacial ice and snow. By this time you are beyond the timber line and well up on the tundra. Just short of Fall River Pass you reach the road's highest point—12,183 feet above sea level. Clammy clouds drift around you, and you may find a driving blizzard sweeping down on you as you dash across the spongy turf to the Alpine Visitor Center and lunch counter. Here if you look sharp you may see the tiny pika that lives only in the high Rockies and betrays his presence to you by comical warning squeaks. Not even the icy climate of the mountaintops can compel the pika to hibernate. Forever hauling grass for its nest, this shy cousin of the rabbit puts up hay just like any lowland farmer.

Beyond Fall River Pass the highway descends in long, sweeping switchbacks to Grand Lake. At Milner Pass, altitude 10,758 feet, you cross the Continental Divide and the Colorado River comes into view. Its source is in the park only a few miles north of the highway. Beyond its valley lies the snow-patched Never Summer Mountains. You follow the valley to the park gate and to the Shadow Mountain National Recreation Area which lies beyond it but is administered by the National Park Service.

This is a memorable trip, but sticking to the park's great highway is only one way of seeing its sights. A better way is to stay a few days at any of the six campgrounds or the many nearby motels. Then get out on the trails into the back country for a closer look. You can hike, ride horses, fish, boat, and sniff that heady highland air. Almost as spectacular as the mountains themselves are their snow-fed lakes and streams, their forests, flowers and wildlife. There are bighorn sheep, ptarmigans, marmot, snowshoe rabbits, marten, and chipmunks; ground squirrels and spruce squirrels can be seen at almost every turn on these high slopes. And as you climb the mountain trails, you can see how the forests and flowers have struggled and adjusted to environments that differ with altitude and exposure. Three such plant zones can be seen in Rocky Mountain National Park—montane, 7,500-9,000 feet; subalpine, 9,000 to about 11,500 feet; and alpine or arctic, above timberline.

In the lowest, or montane zone, where the climate is comparatively warm and dry, the dominant tree is the ponderosa pine. On some cooler, north-facing slopes, the Douglas-fir may mingle with and even displace the ponderosa, but it never attains the great size it does in the Pacific Northwest. The Colorado blue spruce, much admired and widely transplanted, also flourishes at this level. Higher in the montane zone you pass into thick lodgepole pine forests. You also come upon stands of aspen, whose golden leaves in autumn are one of the glories of the park.

At 9,000 feet you find yourself in the sub-alpine zone of plant life, among the kinds of plants that flourish a thousand miles or more to the north in a climate like Canada's. This zone gets about twice as much rain and snow as the one below. When fires and man let it alone, it is dominated

A string of riders crosses Moraine Park, a broad and lovely meadow named for its remarkable glacial deposits.

A trout fisherman wets a line in Fall River. Fishermen need a Colorado license, and the daily limit is ten fish.

by Engelmann spruce and alpine fir. But when fire strikes, as it has around Bear Lake, the forest is slow to recover. First fireweed springs up, then other shrubs like the wax-flower take root. The aspen shoot up next, and then the lodgepole pine. Not for 50 to 70 years, after quick-growing lodgepoles start toppling, does the Engelmann spruce take hold, and the old spruce-fir dominance finally reassert itself. This is the zone of Colorado's state flower, the lovely blue columbine; you will also find it blooming yellow and white amid the glacial rubble.

As you approach 11,000 feet, the spruce and fir grow shorter and more ragged. This borderline level is sometimes called the Hudsonian zone, because of the similarity of its climate to that of Hudson Bay in northern Canada. Not only is it colder at this height but it is much windier, and the loss of water by evaporation is much greater than it would be a thousand feet down the mountainside. Here the most picturesque sight is the limber pine. Near the timber line the limber really lives up to its name, twisting before the wind and pressing against the rocks in the most outlandish shapes. Unfortunately the park's limber pines are menaced by disease; a blister rust that seems to be transmitted by certain valley shrubs the Park Service is now trying to eliminate.

The third, the alpine or arctic zone, is in many ways the most interesting of all. This is the world beyond the timber line, the tundra country, and because of the many flat summits, there are

Male elk may be five feet high, weigh over 600 pounds.

miles of it in Rocky Mountain Park. Here nearly all existing plants are to be found in dwarf form. They bloom in a riot of color that makes the highlands a springy carpet of wildflowers in the month of July. Forced to pack all their growth into a scant five weeks, these tiny plants adjust in weird ways. They shorten stems to conserve growth, and many spin a fine "fur" or tiny hairs along their short stems to hold down evaporation of water by the harsh winter winds.

The wonders of the high Rockies are to be found in every quarter of the park. If you have time by all means take the nine-mile spur that leads through meadows and moraines to summit-shadowed Bear Lake. Behind Bear Lake is fine trail-climbing country—three glaciers, strings of icy, trout-filled lakes, and a couple of all-day hiking and horseback-riding tracks that lead over the Continental Divide toward Grand Lake in one direction and to the slopes of Long's Peak in the other.

Long's Peak is the target for many climbers, and you do not have to be an expert to succeed. You do need good lungs, a pair of stout shoes, and a slicker in case of squalls. You must also leave your name with a ranger beforehand so that someone will be looking for you if you sprain an ankle, and you must not climb alone. The favorite starting point is Long's Peak Camp Ground at the eastern foot near Allenspack Village on State Route 7. You should start at dawn or even earlier so as to be off the summit before afternoon when squalls and sometimes lightning hit the peak. The view from the top is tremendous—great plains rolling away to the eastern horizon, gorges and glacial cirques dropping sharply to ice-green lakes almost at your feet. The trip up and back is an all day scramble but well worth it. The best of Rocky Mountain Park is its wild western scenery, and from Long's Peak you see a splendid example.

Marmots are western cousins of the woodchucks.

Rocky Mountain National Park

N. central Colorado, nr. Estes Park. Area: 395 sq. mi.
Season: June-Sept., roads open year round.
Climate: crisp; elev. 7,800-14,255.
Accommodations: hotels, lodges, campgrounds, trailer sites.
Services: all facilities at Estes Park.
May be reached by major highways.

Badlands National Monument SOUTH DAKOTA

French trappers called it "mauvaises terres." To the Indians it was "mako sica." No matter how you spell it, it means badlands — bad to travel across, terrible to live in, impossible to farm—but good to see, pleasant to visit today, and marvelous as a showcase of our geologic past.

Badlands National Monument, 63 miles east of Rapid City, South Dakota, is an almost unbelievable 170-square-mile treat for the eye. Luckily it is on the main tourist route from the East and Midwest to the Black Hills and Yellowstone, so about a million Americans see it every year. It's a perfect national monument; you can "do" it nonstop by driving its 28-mile scenic highway, or you can make a lifetime study of its paleontology.

Most travelers compromise somewhere between these extremes, then move on to the Black Hills. In Oligocene times, when the Badlands were young and still merely mischievous, the movement was the other way. The enormous uplift of the Black Hills was wearing down and moving as silt, sand, and gravel toward the flat plain. From 40 million to 25 million years ago the sediments collected in a vast marsh. Through rampant vegetation prowled a gallery of fearsome creatures — saber-toothed cats, ancestral camels and pigs, three-toed miniature horses, and giant, grass-eating rhinos called titanotheres.

Then from somewhere came a layer of ash, drifting in from volcanic convulsions. Sluggish, silt-laden streams stopped flowing, the swamp dried up, and the earth's crust lifted. Erosion began its work on the exposed silt—now hardened into clays, shales, and sandstone. Wind and rain created the weird turrets, white pinnacles, and Camelot-like crenellations that jut from lower

Alternating sediments of clay and volcanic ash give Badlands a layercake look. Rain and frost do the slicing.

A paleontologist digs a fossil bone from a gully face.

walls of the tortured landscape. Dry gullies that course with water after spring cloudbursts cut deep into the sediments, exposing layered bands of pastel colors against the distant horizon.

To natural-born, inbred American travelers—who knew all along that the wonders of the world were right here at home—the Badlands are sight-seeing at its best. Your eyes pop, your breath stops, but there they are before you—believe it or not—Tintagel's towers, Taj Mahal's dome, Tenochtitlan's temples, China's Wall, Egypt's Pyramids—all rolled into one.

When you take your eyes off the tumbled and crumbly formations, look into the gully at your feet. There where the chipmunk is scurrying—his feathery tail straight up like a sail—the latest fossil discovery may have been made. For this giddy landscape has its serious side; here the science of vertebrate paleontology began in the United States in the 1840's when the first prehistoric animal bones were discovered.

The best display of extinct Badlands mammals is at Rapid City, in the South Dakota School of Mines. But the monument now boasts an impressive visitor center near Cedar Pass where colorful exhibits tell the Badlands story. Picnicking and camping facilities are available, and on summer evenings, ranger-naturalists give campfire talks.

It was not long before the first fossil find that the Badlands were discovered. Jedediah Smith, the far-ranging pathfinder, traversed the White River country in 1823 and probably became the Badlands' first white sightseer.

In the last, sorry years of the Sioux War, Chief Big Foot was moving his people toward Pine Ridge Reservation. No sightseer, he saw the Badlands as a good place to shake the pursuing Seventh Cavalry. He crossed the desolate barrier by means of a little-known pass (which bears his name today). But the stratagem did not help for long; the cavalry caught him at Wounded Knee, the last major Indian battle in the West, on December 29, 1890.

Since the monument was established in 1939, many visitors have enjoyed it as much for its show of wildflowers and small wildlife as for its scenic grandeur. Chipmunks are everywhere, even in the most barren spots. The amusing little fellows entertain the children while the parents are involved with the horizon.

Ground squirrels, pocket gophers, rabbits, jackrabbits, badgers, and porcupines are numerous. You may glimpse an occasional coyote, deer, or pronghorn. Birds, also, are surprisingly thick.

In the late spring the wildflowers daub the roadsides and gully bottoms with color—phlox, evening primrose, wallflower, yellow sweetpea, loco, mariposa-lily, penstemon, yucca, and prickly pear. The last, a cactus, covers acres with its waxy yellow blooms (but look out for its spines).

Spring is a good time to visit the Badlands. Or fall, to avoid the heat. If you go in summer, try for early morning or late evening, or both. It is cool. The rising and setting sun creates deep shadows and brings out the soft pastel coloring of the strata. Your color pictures will look better than under the flat light of midday.

And don't forget moonlight, and winter. Badlands National Monument is open all the time.

Badlands National Monument

SW South Dakota. Area: 40-mile strip.
Season: year round.
Climate: warm days, cold nights.
Accommodations: Cedar Pass lodge, campground.
Services: visitor center at Cedar Pass.
US Highway 16A leads to park.

Boxwork formations cover Wind Cave's ceiling. Interlacing calcite veins project from a softer limestone base.

Wind Cave National Park SOUTH DAKOTA

Like a gaudy downstairs speakeasy of the Roaring '20's, Wind Cave glitters beneath the somber roof of the Black Hills. Its weird décor, unmatched anywhere in the underworld, features red and brown draperies of lacy calcite, ledges of frostwork, and chandeliers of crystal, and a display of mineral colors set aglow by ultraviolet light.

The calcite boxwork alone is more than worth the modest cover charge. Walls and ceilings are waffled with projecting veins of delicate stone tracery that create mazes of rust-red, criss-crossing, overlapping shadow boxes.

Wind Cave's glories grew slowly. A billion years ago molten granite boiled up and intruded into layers of limestone. (What's left of the granite dome is the Black Hills.) During erosion, ground water dissolved the limestone around the edges, forming underground corridors which further erosion decorated with calcite fantasies.

Tours, April through October, cost 75c for adults (children under 12 free). Park rangers lead groups along one and a quarter miles of lighted passageways that descend 240 feet. Temperature is a constant chilly 47 degrees. Just when you might be tiring of the hike an elevator whisks you to the surface.

A step from the man-made entrance is Wind Cave National Park's greatest oddity—a speleological barometer. This is a 10-inch-wide hole in the ground that connects with the cave. Strong currents of wind blow in and out, a phenomenon caused by changes in atmospheric pressure. Wind blowing out of the cave represents a falling barometer—bad weather. Air whistling in corresponds to a rising barometer, or good weather.

In the early days of settlement, a deer hunter named Tom Bingham discovered Wind Cave when he heard the ground whistling. This was probably the same cave of the winds that the Sioux revered.

The entire Black Hills area, an upland island of trees and rocks and streams in the midst of the dry level Plains, was regarded as sacred by the Sioux. These fierce, cayuse-mounted followers of the buffalo fought a long and bitter war against the white man. Forty-four square miles of their range is here preserved as it was before the heyday of Sitting Bull—complete with buffalo.

Within the boundary fence 350 bison roam free and unattended, perfectly visible from the highway that winds through the park's ponderosa-dotted hills. Not pampered and hay-fed like their cousins in zoos and some other preserves, these shaggy monarchs of the Plains forage at will on the lush grass as did their forebears.

When Europeans arrived in North America, some 60 million bison ranged its grasslands. The Sioux and other Plains Indians got almost everything they needed from buffalo—meat and milk; shields, clothing, moccasins, and blankets from hides; ornaments and utensils from horns; bow strings and thread from sinews. But Indian needs hardly made a dent in the huge herds.

Rifles of the white man were the buffalo's undoing. He killed them for meat, for skins—and for sport. He killed them to clear the Plains for cattle. He killed them to starve the Indians into submission. After the Civil War, the great massacre reached its peak. The slaughter did not stop until there were few buffalos left. A census in 1888 counted only 541 survivors in the United States.

In 1902 the Government started its first captive herd, 21 animals in Yellowstone National Park. It and other herds thrived so well that now more than 5,000 live in U. S. refuges, plus many more thousands in Canada.

Wind Cave's herd shares its range with pronghorn, deer, and elk. Underfoot are prairie dog towns – inhabited by thousands of the comical, darting rodent. When visitors approach their burrows too closely, they whistle or bark a warning—then disappear. But the cantankerous buffalo can't be trusted to warn you that he's dangerous; better watch him from your car.

Wind Cave National Park

SW South Dakota. Area: 44 sq. mi., 10 mi. of passageways.
Season: year round.
Climate: chilly, 47° in cave.
Accommodations: available at Hot Springs, Custer.
Services: visitor center, gift shop, campground.
Park is 10 mi. N of Hot Springs, on US 385.

A herd of bison lives at Wind Cave. A big bull weighs a ton, is fast and shifty, and may be ornery.

)evils Tower National Monument WYOMING

\n 865-foot pillar of rock jutting from the gentle andscape of northeastern Wyoming, Devils Tower ecame the first national monument in September, 906. Aside from its obvious geological fascinaion and scenic beauty, you might suspect that it vas given priority simply because no President ould very well overlook it. You might as well try o ignore a moose in a New York restaurant.

Devils Tower rises with startling abruptness rom beside the Belle Fourche River. There is othing like it in sight, no warning to the motorist f what is to come. Suddenly, there it is—a tapered ylinder with fluted walls, 1,000 feet across at ts base.

To describe Devils Tower in terms of movement s not too imaginative. It once was a molten mass f lava, surging upward from deep in the earth. It ame close to the surface, then cooled and solidied. A million or two years of erosion wore the and away from around this intrusion and left it xposed. Because it cooled slowly, the lava crysallized around the edges, fracturing in a symetrical pattern that produced the strange vertical oints of Devils Tower. These are so straight and ven that from certain angles the great rock looks ke the remnant of a Greek column on a gigantic cale.

At the top of the column is an acre and a half f rock inhabited by birds and, strangely, by ertain mice, pack rats, and chipmunks. The most otable wildlife feature of the monument is the rairie dog town near the base of the tower. These urrowing rodents were once as common a sight n the prairie as the grass itself. Few are left—but eir activities entrance those lucky enough to see em. They live in distinct clans, jealously guard eir boundaries, and show remarkable commuity spirit. As you drive through the dog town you vill see them sitting outside their hummocked urrows, sun-bathing, schooling their young, yaping alarms when intruders get too close. It is this barking that explains their name. They do it so enthusiastically that sometimes they bark themselves over backward.

huge column of splintered basalt, Devil's Tower ands like a gigantic stump above a base of rockfall.

Leaving the prairie dog town, the main road of the monument winds toward the tower and ends at a parking lot near its base. A pleasant trail circles the great nubbin—just over a mile long, and worth every step in its natural history and scenery. But before you follow it, step into the visitor center where displays explain the full meaning of the tower and guide your understanding of its wildlife.

Devils Tower National Monument has a fully equipped campground with facilities for trailers. Follow U.S. 14 west from Rapid City, South Dakota, to near Devils Tower Junction, Wyoming.

Devils Tower National Monument

NE Wyoming. Area: 1,347 acres.
Season: summer months.
Climate: warm days, cool nights.
Accommodations: campgrounds, trailer park.
Services: museum.
US Highway 14, west from Rapid City, S.D. leads to park.

The prairie dog is a large, burrowing rodent.

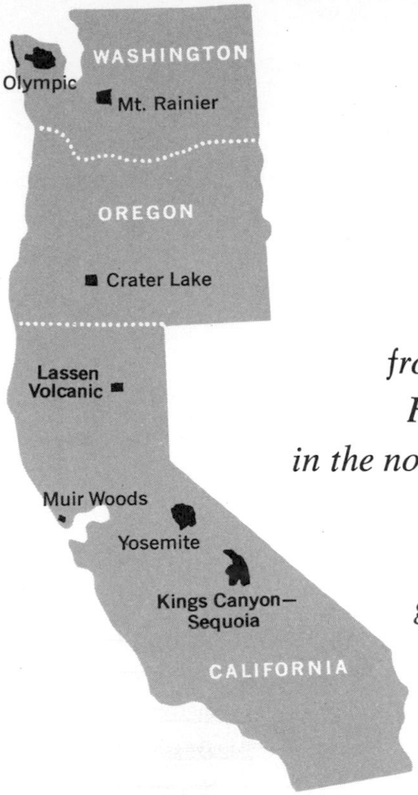

II · THE WEST

In this book the word "West" means the Far West —of California, Oregon and Washington. Variety describes the West, from lush rainforests to snow-topped mountain peaks. Here are the rugged Sierras, and the Cascade Range in the north. Here also are ancient volcanoes and lava flows, canyons, superb waterfalls, valleys sculptured by ice-age glaciers, and the last tracts of America's great virgin forests. The redwoods, fantastic in their size and age, grow only here in all the world, and a long, wild coast, wrapped in mist, stretches for hundreds of miles.

Olympic National Park WASHINGTON

The last region of the nation to be explored was its far northwestern corner. Settlers came late to what is now the state of Washington. And for decades the townsfolk of Seattle looked across Puget Sound at the Olympic range—snowy peaks gleaming mysteriously between veils of cloud—and wondered what kind of land lay there. Not until the late 19th century did two expeditions cut across the Olympic Peninsula and find out. "While the country on the outer slope of these mountains is valuable," reported one explorer, "the interior is useless for all practicable purposes. It would, however, serve admirably for a national park." And so, at last, it does.

Olympic National Park wasn't established until 1938. Then the park service took over a large area of true wilderness—a tangle of peaks draped with glaciers; deep, broad valleys smothered in forest; a land rich in wildlife and incredibly endowed with plants and trees.

Rain forest lies on the western slope of the Olympic Mountains where moist winds deliver a steady drizzle.

Even the influx of eager tourists has not upset the reign of wild nature in the park. There are no roads across the 1,400-square-mile tract, though several roads enter it. The Olympic elk bugles from the high ridges and the great trees of the rain forests creak and sigh in the wind as they have for centuries, without the crack of the rifle or the snarl of the chain saw to disturb them.

Along the valleys of the Quinault, Queets, and Hoh rivers are the finest coniferous rain forests to be found in the temperate zones of the earth. The western slope of the mountains, where these streams flow, is drenched by about 12 feet of rain each year. There are many days of light rain, from September to May—and occasional heavy downpours. Summers are mostly clear. This vast steady rainfall, along with the rather mild climate of the Pacific coast, produces the right conditions for remarkable forest growth.

Down in the low-lying, humid valleys, western hemlock, Sitka spruce, and Douglas fir reach gigantic proportions, their upper branches blocking out the sky. These trees thrive in the shade, yet can speed their rate of growth to fill a gap in the forest ceiling caused by the toppling of some over-age giant. And topple they do in winter storms. Not only is growth faster here, but death comes more quickly, and rot and decay is rampant, ever making way for the new growth. So the rain forest remains a solidly matted mass of evergreen.

Vine maples and shrubs form the "understory" of the forest. Mosses smother logs on the forest floor, the understory trees, the great straight trunks and massive branches of the big trees. The result is a fantastic world of soft carpeted forest groves, each curtained by its own draperies. Only a little light filters down from the 200-foot-high tree tops. But since green moss festoons many surfaces, the light itself turns green, rather than gloomy. It bounds downward, from trunk to branch to leaf to floor, giving a feeling of mystery to these silent halls and corridors within the rain forest.

Silent? At first, yes, the forest world seems soundless, as though no hint of noise had ever managed to penetrate its thickly padded recesses. But as you stand among the trees, alone and listening, you will suddenly hear the constant low-pitched voice of the forest itself. There is the wind, of course, far overhead, sighing and whispering. And often there is the cello note of one branch rubbing against another. The cheery song of the winter wren, or the tapping of a pileated woodpecker breaks the woodland silence.

The rain forest teems with life, but it is either on a microscopic or gigantic scale. You may hear, for example, the distant crash of a tree falling. Soon after it touches the forest floor tiny organisms begin the process of reducing and digesting that shattered trunk. Before long a seed will lodge in its mossy carcass, then another and another until the rotting giant is a "nursery" for seedlings, especially of hemlock and Sitka spruce, trees that prefer to take root in wood. The forest has many examples of well-grown trees standing in a straight line as though planted by hand. They weren't. It's just that they all were nurtured by the same ancient nurse log, now crumbled away in the forest duff. Seedlings, after gaining a foothold in a decaying log, often shoot their roots down around the dead form and into the ground. When the old log finally rots away the living tree is left standing on stilts.

The magic of the rain forest is enough to en-

A bear and her cubs await a handout. Only black-coated species live in Olympic National Park.

Mist swirls about the Olympic peaks. The range seems loftier than it is because it rises from sea level.

trance a visitor for all of his stay at Olympic National Park. But there is much more to see. Above the valleys are the ridges—whalebacks of mountain meadow rich in wildflowers and magnificent in their views of the jumbled summits. These mountains aren't very high by western standards. Mount Olympus itself, the biggest on the peninsula, is only 7,965 feet. But they rise from near sea level and seem huge. Glaciers carved their shapes, left grassy cirques on their flanks, scoured and rounded their valleys, and still inch downward from their heights. Glacial melt streams down to nourish the west-flowing rivers and eventually foam into the sea. And from the sea comes that staggering rainfall which feeds the low forests and, in the form of heavy snow, builds up the glaciers again.

One park road leads up Hurricane Ridge, the favorite vantage point for a view of the Olympics. You can take this road at Port Angeles, just north of the park, and follow it past park headquarters, with a pause at the visitor center. Most of the choice regions within the park are all the better for their remoteness. You must take to the trails—there are about 600 miles of them—to appreciate this wilderness thoroughly. Pack horses are available at Sol Duc Hot Springs in the northwest corner of the park. Keep an eye peeled for the magnificent dark-maned Roosevelt elk, for deer and bear. When you are startled by a piercing whistle some late afternoon as you are making camp on a high meadow, don't look for a strong-lunged human being. It's a marmot, a fat, cheerful western cousin of the woodchuck, who lives among the rocks and whistles to warn his neighbors of danger.

The park has many campgrounds within its borders. Kalaloch (pronounced "clay-lock") campground, built to handle big house trailers lies next to the ocean. Evening campfire talks by rangers are held right on the beach. Campgrounds remain open all year in the valleys. But the high country remains closed from the first snowfall, around

Climbers study a crevasse. They walk well-spaced and roped together; the snow may often cover deep cracks.

early November, until early June. Port Angeles is the place to head for. Here are many motels, park headquarters and a visitor center. Accommodations are also available at Lake Crescent and other spots around the peninsula.

If you are a fisherman, Olympic offers five kinds of trout in its streams and lakes. You need a Washington license for certain areas. If you seek mountains to climb, you'll find them here. Some peaks are only for experts who have equipment for glacier and rock climbing. Mountaineers must register before starting.

But Olympic is more than an inland park endowed with forest and mountain scenery. One of its great surprises is the Ocean Strip, a narrow coastline 50 miles long that was added to the park in 1953. It is perhaps the wildest stretch of seashore in the nation. Rocky points clad in evergreen punctuate crescents of gray

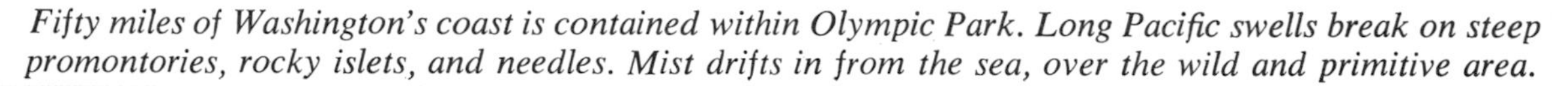

Fifty miles of Washington's coast is contained within Olympic Park. Long Pacific swells break on steep promontories, rocky islets, and needles. Mist drifts in from the sea, over the wild and primitive area.

Avalanche lilies cover a high meadow with star-shaped flowers. They bloom in mid-summer up to timberline.

beach. Chunky rock islets stand just offshore. Big trees, swept seaward in floods, end up as driftwood along the Ocean Strip. Deer wander down to lick salt. Even elk appear, and bear are rather common here.

At three places along the strip are Indian reservations where coastal tribesmen live their own lives and earn their livings by salmon fishing. They still make the finest dugout canoes of any Indians in the United States. You can run down part of the Quinault River in one for a modest fee.

One experience you should try on the Ocean Strip is to follow the Indian custom of dipping smelt from the surf with nets. Rangers will show you how to do it, and you can rent a dip net at Ruby Beach, which lies just south of the Hoh Indian Reservation.

Olympic National Park

NW Washington. Area: 1,400 sq. mi.

Season: campgrounds open year round, high roads July-Nov.

Climate: cool summers, cold winters.

Accommodations: campgrounds, lodges, hotels.

Services: visitor center.

Route 101, west of Port Angeles, leads to park. Ferry acr. Puget Sound and Hood Canal.

Mount Rainier National Park WASHINGTON

"Major scenic wonder," "natural masterpiece," "striking landmark of the Pacific Northwest"—in such phrases writers describe Mount Rainier National Park in south-central Washington. All of these enthusiasms are apt. The great mountain and its surrounding country are unquestionably among the most impressive and beautiful sights in North America—a splendid harmony of peak and flowering meadow, still lakes, flowing streams, and deep forest.

Mount Rainer rises 14,410 feet above sea level and is the highest mountain in the Cascade Range. Its summit, always snowclad, towers nearly two miles above its foothills. But more impressive than its height is its massive beauty. Volcanic in origin, it was built up by lava flows and eruptions of cinder and ash after the recent geologic age which saw the formation of the Cascade Range, which lies eastward. Rainier's crest is not a sharp peak but, like many other volcanoes, has a more domed top, an undulating snow-covered expanse about one mile square.

This summit area is marked by three separate peaks, the Columbia Crest on the east being the highest, and by the rims of two distinct volcanic craters. The smaller crater still has active steam vents which melt the snow in their vicinity. These steam vents remind us that Rainier is part of the great Pacific "ring of fire," the double chain of volcanoes that stretches up the west coast of the Americas, curves along the coastline of Asia, then dips into the Indian Ocean. Somewhere along this chain of volcanoes there is always activity. A number of volcanic eruptions have occurred in modern times.

Don't let this scare you away from Mount Rainier. Except for those steam vents, it has been quiet for centuries.

When Mount Rainier was born, it had the smooth, contoured slopes of the typical volcanic cone—Fujiyama, for example—but today its sides are remarkable for the deep canyons and sharp ridges that have been gouged by water and glaciers. Some glaciation dates back to the last Ice Age, but Rainier does very well at making and maintaining its own great rivers of ice. There are, in fact, 26 active glaciers on Rainier's flanks which cover about 40 square miles. They come down on all sides, for Rainier's shape is still roughly conical, and they form one of the most impressive displays of glacial ice anywhere. Twelve of them originate in or near the summit and extend well below timberline to elevations of about 5,000 feet. The Emmons Glacier, five miles long and one mile wide, is the largest. It and the Nisqually are the best known and most easily visited of these major ice flows.

Little wonder Mount Rainier has so many glaciers. Glacial ice is formed from pressure of

Rainier's blunted cone towers over Nisqually Glacier, which pokes its icy snout deep into Paradise Valley.

layer after layer of snow, deep and packed hard by its own weight. Rainier, thrusting upward in this moist Northwest climate, intercepts this moisture and nearly 50 feet of snow falls each year in Paradise Valley on the mountain's southern flank. This snow is finally compressed into glacier ice. On the surface, the glacier flows about 25 feet a month. In the summer and at lower elevations, the glaciers begin to melt and pour water into the park's many streams and creeks. In many places the melt water plunges abruptly and dramatically into glacier-cut valleys whence the ice has now retreated.

In glowing, lively contrast to these impressive but barren tongues of ice are the alpine meadows which surround the mountain. In the late spring and summer a belt of mountain wildflowers circles the peak where there are neither dense forests nor glaciers, at altitudes between 5,000 and 6,000 feet. Here you may find a wide variety of the plants typical of what is known as the Hudsonian zone, so named because this plant community resembles that at the southern end of Hudson Bay. A man climbing to this zone has traveled the equivalent, botanically speaking, of hundreds of miles north into Canada. Although hidden by snowdrifts the major portion of the year, these slopes are covered with plants that bloom suddenly, intensely and very colorfully as soon as the snow is gone, to take maximum advantage of the short growing season.

Skiing is excellent December to May. There are rope tows at the inn, but no overnight accommodations.

Mountain flowers bloom in wild profusion during the short summer months.

Above this Hudsonian zone of vegetation and above the treeline are meadows which the botanists classify as Arctic-Alpine. Here may be found plants typical of all the high mountain areas of North America—stunted plants and bushes and ground-hugging cushion plants which survive the rigors of their cold and wind-swept environment by clinging close to the ground and seeking shelter in the lee of rocks. In the Sunrise area, near Frozen Lake, is one of the most beautiful of these natural rock gardens. In all, more than 700 species of flowering plants grow on the slopes of Mount Rainier.

At lower elevations the flanks of the mountain are clothed with heavy stands of some of the world's most beautiful and impressive trees. Forests of western hemlock, Douglas-fir and western redcedar are so thick and luxuriant that their branches interlace overhead and produce, even on bright summer days, a hushed twilight on the forest floor. At about 3,500 feet elevation these forests give way to equally impressive stands of Pacific silver fir, Alaska yellowcedar, noble fir and western white pine.

In forests and upland meadows live a wide variety of animals. Bear and deer are common, and even mountain goats, those agile and elusive climbers, can be seen at high elevations during the summer. Elk have recently moved into the southeastern portion of the park. Small animals like raccoons, ground squirrels and marmots abound, as do their predators—coyotes, bobcats, and a few mountain lions. The wildlife is abundant and easily observed because hunting in the park is forbidden.

To help visitors see and appreciate its natural wonders the park has an excellent system of roads, trails, and camping sites. Park naturalists give illustrated talks in the evenings during the summer at Paradise, Ohanapecosh, Sunrise and Longmire. A schedule of guided walks is posted on park bulletin boards, and professional guide service is available for summit trips at Paradise.

It's a hard climb to Mount Rainier's ice fields and glaciers, and if you wish to try for the summit you must have a guide or satisfy the rangers that your party has an experienced leader and proper equipment.

An ice cave tunnels under Paradise Glacier. Warm drafts of air enlarge the tunnel and sunlight, penetrating the ice, tints the cave blue. Rainier has 26 glaciers; one is five miles long.

Of the 300 miles of trails in the park, 90 make up the Wonderland Trail which completely circles the mountain. Campsites and shelter cabins are spaced eight to 12 miles apart on this fine trail and allow a determined hiker to be comfortable by night while still passing through some truly primitive wilderness. If you're a fisherman, shorter trails will take you to clear streams and lakes where good catches can be made late in the season. Fishing regulations are posted at all of the Ranger Stations in the park.

Mount Rainier National Park
S-central Washington. Area: 378 sq. mi.
Season: climbing, June-Labor Day, reg. May-Oct.
Climate: cool days, cold nights.
Accommodations: cabins.
Route 5 leads into park.

A newborn fawn lies still when alarmed. As he grows, his spots will disappear and then he will run from danger.

Crater Lake National Park OREGON

According to legends of the Klamath Indians, a great mountain now called Mazama once stood on the site of Oregon's Crater Lake. From his throne on Mazama's summit the "Chief of the Below World" warred with the "Chief of the Above World," who stood atop Mount Shasta more than a hundred miles to the south. For seven days, the story goes, rock and flame and terrible explosions rent the blackened sky, destroying forests and the Indians' villages. Then Mount Mazama caved in on itself.

Following Crater Lake's discovery by prospectors in 1853, scientists held for many years that its bowl was the shattered base of a mountain that had literally "blown its top." But geologic evidence recently led them to an explanation remarkably similar to the Indians'—that some 6,600 years ago a volcano more than two miles high had collapsed into the vast empty chamber from which its lava had spewed. Indian artifacts have been found in areas surrounding the Park, covered by ash and pumice from Mount Mazama's climax eruptions, suggesting that the ancestors of today's Klamaths had witnessed the fall of Mount Mazama. Their legend, at any rate, had been handed down by word of mouth for over six thousand years.

Just as unusual was the size of Mazama's lava chamber. It was wide enough and deep enough to swallow an estimated 15½ cubic miles of the mountain's bulk, and leave a caldera six miles across and three-quarters of a mile deep. Rain and snow gradually filled the cavity. Today Crater Lake goes down 1,932 feet at its deepest, and yet it reaches barely halfway up the caldera's highest cliffs. Equal in area to the island of Manhattan, the lake's startlingly blue surface is broken only by Wizard Island, a cinder cone that extends 774 feet above it, and Phantom Ship, a sliver of rock that looks from the distance like a galleon under full sail.

Lying athwart the volcanic Cascade Range, the 250 square miles of Crater Lake National Park contain many other displays of volcanism. The Pumice Desert covers a broad stretch of upland with packed lava dust up to 200 feet deep. Giant spikes of lava poke up from the canyons of Wheeler Creek and Annie Creek. They are the solidified cores of gas vents now exposed by erosion. Several volcanic dikes — walls of molten rock that welled up through cracks and then hardened — have also been left standing in the caldera as surrounding earth washed away. Old lava flows can be seen on the floors of U-shaped valleys scoured out by even more ancient glaciers.

A steep beach edges Crater Lake's clear water. The sheer, black cliffs rise abruptly around the lake's shores

Except for Pumice Desert, vegetation has reclaimed most of the park's devastated areas. In three distinct "life zones" grow more than 570 species of fern and flowering plants. Forests of fir, hemlock and pine rise from rolling meadows. Small animals are numerous and varied: the red fox, the black bear, the pika or rock-rabbit crying from its cranny in a talus slope; the eagle, raven ınd peregrine falcon wheeling above the caldera.

But the lake itself is the chief attraction. For ıside from its geologic interest only one word de- ıcribes it, and that word is beautiful. The un- ›elievable blue comes from the way the clear vater absorbs light. All the colors of the sun's pectrum penetrate far down into the pure and ransparent water. Only the deepest of blues re- ›ounds from the depths, and emerging, strikes he eye. Sometimes the surface is still as a mirror ınd carries the inverted image of the far shore ınd the distant drifting clouds. Then a catspaw of ›reeze streaks the face of the indigo lake with a ›right stain of silver.

Though the water is pure, it is not lifeless. It ıas a population of salamanders, crayfish and resh-water shrimp. Rainbow trout and kokanee almon have been introduced and thrive.

A good road circles the rim. Parking turnouts nd trails offer a variety of views. Boats may be ented for sightseeing or fishing, or you may fish rom the shore. Daily limit is ten fish. There are our free campgrounds, or you can stay at Crater ˌake Lodge. Make reservations early: 3185 SW 7th Avenue, Portland, Oregon. Season is June 15 hrough September, depending on snow conditions. Paved state highways connect the park's road system with U.S. 97, 99, 101, and 199.

HOW CRATER LAKE WAS FORMED

Molten lava rose into the throat and flank vents of Mount Mazama. The lava, heavily charged with dissolved gas, foamed like a colossal bottle of warm pop. About 10 cubic miles of frothy lava shot out of the volcano's throat in great swirling clouds and drifted down in the form of pumice, ash and cinders. As the last of the molten material subsided deep into the earth, Mazama, its old flanks weakened, collapsed into its feeding chamber, forming the great caldera, six miles wide and 4,000 feet deep. This pit is now half-filled with the blue waters of Crater Lake.

Crater Lake National Park

S-central Oregon. Area: 160,000 acres.
Season: July-Sept.
Climate: cold.
Accommodations: campgrounds, Crater Lake Lodge.
Services: boats, fishing.
US highways 97, 99, 101, and 199 lead to park.

Wizard Island is a cinder cone built up in recent times. Inset shows the probable original profile of Mt. Mazama.

Lingering snow blankets Lassen peak in early summer. Manzanita Lake may be seen in the foreground.

Lassen Volcanic National Park CALIFORNIA

Steel-blue lakes, flower-bright meadows, timbered slopes, high trails winding over hills carpeted with chaparral—California's Lassen Park has all these in its 165 square miles of rugged terrain. But it is the work of volcanoes that gives the park distinction. From its lowliest mud pot, bubbling away in a rocky hollow, to the steaming crater of 10,457-foot Lassen peak, the park is a museum of volcanic activity.

Everywhere a visitor sees reminders of the awesome forces that are now quiet below the surface. Around Lassen Peak lie the weathered skeletons of trees knocked down by a great gaseous blast in 1915; 20-ton boulders swept downslope by powerful mudflows can be found more than five miles from their former resting places. To the north stand the jagged Chaos Crags, which took shape as stiff lava was forced up through vents. Avalanches from these crags skated across a slippery base of wet volcanic ash, forming Chaos Jumbles—about two and a half square miles of rocky rubble. Around Cinder Cone, standing wit superb symmetry some 10 miles east of Lasse Peak, spread multi-colored dunes, thick beds o lava, and rough piles of volcanic slag.

Just to the south of Lassen Peak lies Bumpas Hell, a broad area still seething with volcani heat: steaming fumaroles, hissing hot spring gurgling mud pots, crystal-lined "solfataras," a mineralized "River Styx," and a cauldron c volcanic rock scooped out by hot acids. Othe thermal areas include Sulphur Works, Devi Kitchen, Little Hot Springs Valley, and Boilin Springs Lake.

The park's most spectacular volcanic feature i the snow-clad mountain that gave it its nam Lassen Peak is the southernmost and most recentl active of the great volcanic mountains of the Ca cade Range. It began life long ago as a small ver on the flank of a much larger volcano known a Mount Tehama, which geologists say was a fu two miles high and twelve miles wide at its bas with a crater more than 3,000 feet in diameter. Sometime in the prehistoric past Mount Tehama collapsed leaving a vast bowl-like caldera. The eroded rim is still marked by Brokeoff Mountain, Mount Diller, Mount Conard, and the base of Pilot Pinnacle.

Meanwhile Lassen Peak grew enormously over the centuries. Layer on layer of lava built up its walls. Then a great mass of stiff lava was driven up through its crater by the tremendous pressure from below. This mass hardened into a towering mound of solid rock—a huge "plug dome"—and Lassen entered a long period of quiet.

The peak's latest series of eruptions began on May 30, 1914. A year later a red tongue of lava poured out of its new crater, and melting snow sent streams of hot mud flowing down into the valleys of Lost Creek and Hat Creek. Three days later the mountain erupted violently spewing clouds of debris five miles into the sky. A stupendous gas explosion roared northeastward, felling huge pines as far as three miles away. Then, its energy spent, the activity slowly died away over the next few years.

For centuries the area that in 1916 became Lassen Volcanic National Park was the hunting and camping grounds of four Indian tribes. These four tribes probably contained 4,000 Indians in

Volcanic steam blasts from the ground at Bumpass Hell.

1776, but by 1950 their number had dwindled to 350. Indian exhibits at the visitor center tell about how they lived. You can also purchase a booklet telling the remarkable Indian story including that of Ishi (which means "I Am a Man"), the last of the Yahis, who died in 1921. The peak was named in 1856 after Peter Lassen, a Danish guide who used it as a landmark while leading emigrants from Nevada into northern California.

For all its fireworks, Lassen Volcanic National Park remains a green place, a lush, unspoiled

Chaos Crags are hardened plugs of lava pushed up in a stiff state. Rockfall litters the foreground.

Cinder Cone, in northeast part of the park, was landmark of the old emigrant trail which skirts its base.

wilderness. The crimson snow plant, the bleeding heart, the monkey flower and the leopard lily grow in vivid clusters on mountain meadows. Pine, alder, aspen, willow and cottonwood stand thick on the slopes. The waters are stocked with rainbow, brown, and eastern brook trout. More than a hundred species of birds, from the humming bird and mourning dove to the mountain quail and the kingly bald eagle, make Lassen their home. Among the animals are friendly ground squirrels, red foxes, black bears, mule deer, and Columbian blacktail deer.

Spring comes late to Lassen's snowy uplands. Good skiing often lasts into July, and even in midsummer the night air has an autumnal snap and chill. Lake and stream fishing is good in September and October. Accommodations are comfortable in two guest lodges. There are several free campgrounds within the park area.

Park services include an Indian program, illustrated campfire nature talks, walks, hikes led by ranger-naturalists, and a fascinating museum at Manzanita Lake. The park's main roads are good, its side roads at least passable, and its five self-guiding nature trails excellent. The park lies less than 150 miles north of Sacramento. State highway 89 runs through it and may be reached by way of U.S. 99 and State Routes 36 and 44.

Lassen Volcanic National Park

N California. Area: 166 sq. mi.
Season: May-Oct.
Climate: nights cold.
Accommodations: lodges, campgrounds.
Services: Indian program, nature talks, hikes, museum

A Columbian Blacktail deer fawn stands poised for flight. After a few months he will lose his baby spots.

Raccoons usually spend their days in hollow trees, going out at night to hunt mice, frogs, eggs, and fruit.

Muir Woods National Monument

CALIFORNIA

Muir Woods is small—only 510 acres. There is nothing much to do here, just walk through the forest. It makes no demands on you except simple response to beauty—its great trees, the delicate things that grow beneath them, and the misty softness of the air itself. It is a place for contemplation, not for strenuous activity. The woods lie just a few miles across the Golden Gate Bridge from San Francisco. Come early and you will have the place to yourself. In silence you can walk along Redwood Creek, the dark brown trunks rising all around you and stretching up to the forest's roof, half lost in the mist.

Their height makes the trees seem to converge, to lean over you like curious giants. They are *sequoia sempervirens,* tallest on earth. One of them, in a California state park, held the world's record at 364 feet. The coast redwoods here at Muir Woods are no record breakers, but they tower well over 200 feet, high enough to give you a stiff neck from looking up. This, moreover, is a virgin forest. If you hear the crash of a falling branch during your solitary walk, it is not the work of an ax. Only nature prunes these trees.

The coast redwood is darker in color than its huge cousin, the giant sequoia found in Yosemite and Sequoia national parks. It also is slimmer; the largest example at Muir Woods is 14 feet through, less than half the diameter of the General Sherman tree at Sequoia. Redwoods often grow from big humpy burls, bulging from the base of parent trunks. Several may sprout from the roots of a tree killed by fire, slowly growing up around the old stump. Finally they stand in a group of partial circles. Such a group may live 1,500 years.

Muir Woods once belonged to California Congressman William Kent. He and his wife realized the commercial threat to redwoods early in this century and gave this forested valley to the United States. They suggested that it be named after President Theodore Roosevelt's old friend, John Muir.

Coast redwoods rise straight as a mast above tanbark trail. Sunlight barely penetrates their lofty crowns.

Muir was perhaps the most extraordinary naturalist, conservationist, and just plain adventurer the West has ever known. Packing little except some salt and a loaf of bread, he explored the Sierras, plunged into the Alaskan wilderness, laid out trails, discovered glaciers, climbed peaks, and lived for months with only the trees overhead. A small, tough man, he never shaved, never got sick in the woods, and was never attacked by an animal or snake. His secret: make lots of noise as you go. When he wanted to observe the wildlife, he sat quietly, letting the animals come to him.

He wrote ferocious articles to save his wilderness. In many ways he was as much of a giant as the trees that are now his monument.

Muir Woods is open from sunrise to sunset, and is a fine place to walk and picnic in designated areas. Camping and fires are not permitted.

Muir Woods National Monument

California, N of San Francisco. Area: 485 acres.
Season: daytime, year round.

Yosemite National Park CALIFORNIA

"GO WEST, YOUNG MAN!" was advice that Horace Greeley handed out freely back in the 19th century. The best of the West, he said, after taking a look, was the green-golden land of California's High Sierras. "They surpass any mountains I ever saw," said editor Greeley.

You will find the richest sights and delights of the High Sierra in California's oldest, most famous and most popular park, Yosemite. If you like forests, it has three groves of giant sequoias and whole mountainsides of evergreens ("I never enjoyed such a tree feast," said old Horace Greeley). If you want mountains, its skyline includes such peaks as Mt. Lyell (13,114 ft.) and Mt. Dana (13,053 ft.). If you like hiking or horseback riding, the park's "high country" is laced with hundreds of miles of wilderness trails.

But the sight of sights is stupendous Yosemite Valley itself, seven miles long and a mile wide on the average, flanked by sheer granite monoliths greater than the rock of Gibraltar and waterfalls 10 times higher than Niagara.

You view this spectacle from Glacier Point; you feel the ground shake in spring as those torrents hurtle 1,500 feet to the valley floor; and ask: how did all this come to be? Geologists tell us that three great forces shaped Yosemite—the birth of the mountains, the work of the glaciers, and the ruggedness of the foundation rock itself.

Once, the valley's Merced River was a sluggish stream drifting slowly past low ridges to the Pacific. Then, about 100 million years ago, a great block of the earth's crust thrust steeply upward to form the Sierra Nevada mountains. Down this great block's long westward slope toward what is now the San Joaquin Valley of California rushed the Merced River, sluggish no longer. Swift and vigorous, the river cut itself a canyon 2,000 feet deep. But the little side tributaries, without any such tilt to speed their descent, flowed much as they had before. So the Merced cut deep and they were left high above. The results are still to be seen today in the "hanging valleys" of such streams as Bridalveil, Sentinel, Ribbon and Yosemite creeks and the plumes of water that plunge and tumble from them into Yosemite Valley itself.

The glaciers have entered the Yosemite scene only in the last million years. You can follow their

Wawona Tree in Mariposa Grove, cut through in 1881 to impress stagecoach tourists, is still alive and healthy.

From the brow of Half Dome, Tenaya Creek, a mile below, stretches away toward Yosemite's high country.

Mariposa Grove stands silent in winter's deep snow. The Badger Pass ski area and Valley roads remain open.

traces as they pushed and ground down Tenaya, Illilouette and Merced canyons into Yosemite Valley, packing the valley from wall to wall, making it U-shaped instead of V-shaped, and carving the walls themselves into weird pinnacles, spires, domes and arches. The mighty glacial stairs they cut as they advanced and receded are clearly to be seen in the upper river beds. Vernal and Nevada Falls are two such stairs 317 and 594 feet high in the upper course of the Merced; above each of them is a hollow, or tread, that once held a lake. Of the three great glaciers that thrust at different times into Yosemite Valley, one was stopped by the mighty shoulders of El Capitan on one side and Cathedral Rocks on the other, and the second pushed through almost to El Portal at the west entrance to the park. The last and smallest of the glaciers gave Yosemite Valley its parklike floor. Receding, it left a rocky moraine big enough to dam its melting waters and create ancient Lake Yosemite, which covered the valley from wall to wall. Silt washing down from the Sierra then gradually filled up this lake too, creating the flower-flecked meadowlands you see today. And in the high country above the valley lie dozens of sparkling lakes, filling the hollows scoured out by the great ice sheet that fed the valley glaciers. Here, too, are meadows of hip-deep grass, each one an ancient lake that silted in. Flat slopes of smooth granite, rubbed smooth by the great pressing palm of the glaciers still carry a glistening sheen. "Glacial polish," they call it.

The third force that shaped Yosemite was the granite itself that rose from the very heart of the earth to make the mountains. Where it pushed up in solid masses, such domes as El Capitan and Sentinel Rock were left jutting skyward even after less tough rock had weathered away. Where the cracks or cleavage joints were vertical, great slabs of stone were more easily torn away, leaving sheer cliffs. Where the joints were curved, you get the domes that resisted the splitting and scaling action of water and ice. This is now the scientifically accepted explanation of Half Dome, the great rock that rises 4,800 feet at the upper end of Yosemite Valley. One side of Half Dome is formed with a vertical system of joints, the other side with curved. So its surface on one side was split away

Bridalveil Creek plummets 620 feet from its hanging valley, then threads its way to the Merced River.

A string of riders heads out across the high country, a thousand square miles of stunning, uncrowded scenery.

in chunks by glaciers leaving it flat, but on the other it has been rounded by gradual scaling or flaking off of slabs of rock by frost and water.

One day, by this process, the famous overhang of Half Dome must crack and fall a clear half mile to its sloping base, and then go crashing down the slope itself, far into the head of the valley. But the rangers at Yosemite tell you this won't happen in your time or your children's time or for a long time after that. Meanwhile an eight-mile trail with 900 feet of hand cables will lead you to one of the world's most stupendous views at the top of the dome.

Of our great mountain parks, Yosemite is the nearest to big cities—only 195 miles from San Francisco, 313 miles from Los Angeles. The valley has a hotel, two lodges, and six campgrounds in its eight square miles of floor, and is crowded in the summer months. But away from the valley floor, out in the back country, you can find all the room in the world. After all, the park has 1,182 square miles of magnificent forested mountain country—

El Capitan, a flawless granite monolith, juts three-quarters of a mile straight up from the valley floor.

plenty of room for every visitor. Within an hour's walk from any road you will find solitude as beautiful and profound as the first white explorers discovered early in the 19th century.

Tuolumne Meadows on the new, wide Tioga Pass Road is a center for high country trails. The rangers say: "Those of you who walk will probably wish you had ridden and those of you who ride will wish you had walked." Along these well-marked High Sierra trails are tent camps so spotted that you can find a bed and meal at the end of the day for $6.00 and so avoid having to carry a pack. Fishing is good around the Vogelsang, Tuolumne Meadows and Glen Aulin High Sierra camps. Write the Yosemite Park and Curry Company, Yosemite National Park, California, for information. This company will describe all the various accommodations, ranging from the luxurious (and expensive) Ahwahnee Hotel in Yosemite Valley to the reasonable (and camplike) tent cabins. There are 18 campgrounds in the park. Those in the valley are open from mid-May to

The trail to Half Dome approaches from the rear. Final stretch is a pair of cables fastened to sheer granite.

High country hotel: commercial camps, spotted along trails, supply bedding and meals for overnight hikers.

mid-September, those in the high country open a little later, as the snow melts off.

Warning: Yosemite has about 20,000 deer and plenty of bears. *Don't feed them!* It makes them dependent on hand-outs, and unable to cope with nature's demands. It also makes them so greedy as to be dangerous to humans. Deer may slash with their sharp hoofs, bears may claw and bite without the slightest warning. As for snakes, yes, there are some rattlers at Yosemite. Follow the advice of John Muir who spent a lifetime tramping through the Sierras without any gun—or any trouble: Make plenty of noise in the wilderness and animals will leave you alone.

Tips: The Tioga Pass road east from the park is one of the most spectacular mountain roads in the United States. Every night at 9 there is a "fire-fall" from the Glacier Point that is one of the sights of a Yosemite summer. Dancing is nightly at the Ahwahnee Hotel. The falls run full in the early summer when the snow melts, but by August most have shrunk to a trickle.

Yosemite National Park

Central California. Area: 1,189 sq. mi.
Season: year round.
Climate: summer days pleasant, nights cool.
Accommodations: hotels, lodges, cabins, tents.
Services: visitor center, nature center, horses.
State Highways 140, 41, 120. Trailers allowed over Tioga Pass at night only. Closed winters.

Seen from Glacier Point, the Merced River rushes past Liberty Cap, then plunges headlong over Nevada and Vernal Falls and continues its swift seaward journey.

Sequoia and Kings Canyon National Parks CALIFORNIA

Against the grandeur of a mountain backdrop stand the largest living things in the world: the giant sequoia trees of California. Awed Indians "walked in silence" among them. Modern Americans, just as awed and reverent, have preserved many thousands of the trees in Sequoia National Park, the second oldest in the National Park System. Sequoia and its neighbor, Kings Canyon National Park, embrace 1,314 square miles of rugged Sierra Nevada wilderness and over 25 sequoia forests.

Nearly a million visitors come annually to see the big trees of Giant Forest, the largest grove. They picnic or camp in it or stay in rustic cabins, and walk the trails which wind among this cathedral of trees.

If you approach Sequoia Park from Visalia and Three Rivers and drive up the Generals Highway that winds through groves in both parks, you will be following the route of the first white man to see the big trees: rancher Hale Tharp. Indians led him up twisting trails to show him the wonder in 1858.

The route is a smooth highway now, but you will swing around many a hairpin turn as your car climbs more than a mile. The canyon of the Kaweah River, yawning below you, and the distant snowy peaks of the Great Western Divide will give you a taste of the high country ahead.

The air will be cool in the 6,000-foot altitude when you see the first sequoias, their cinnamon-red bark standing out among the trunks of the smaller white firs and sugar pines.

That reddish bark and the awl-like needles of the evergreen are among the characteristics that distinguish the giant sequoia from its cousin, the coast redwood. Though both are often called redwood, the giant sequoia is a different tree, not as tall (coast redwoods average about 50 feet taller) but a good deal bulkier.

It is the heavyweight champion without any doubt. The champion of all is the General Sherman, named for the Union general of Civil War fame. With a diameter of 36½ feet at the base and tapering only slightly for half its height of 272 feet, the tree has been estimated to weigh in the neighborhood of 2,000 tons and to contain enough wood to build a 40-house village. Its main limbs are bigger than most trees.

The General Sherman is situated among so many other big trees and is so well proportioned that its size can be deceptive. To realize fully the enormity of this giant, picture your house standing nearby, and pace off its dimensions. The Sherman is as wide as most streets, and if it were tunneled like the Wawona Tree in Yosemite National Park, not one but three cars abreast could drive through it.

But size is not the only characteristic to ponder when you visit the giant sequoias. Think of their age—nearly 4,000 years, some of them! They are among the oldest living things on earth. Only the bristle-cone pines have been proved older, and the sequoias may have a longer life span, for no one

General Sherman Tree, center, ranks as the largest living thing on earth. Yard-thick bark is resistant to fire.

Red flowers of Hygrophorus brighten the forest floor.

Fishing is fine in the park. Nearby lakes harbor trout, whose golden color protects them in the sun-flecked water.

has found a sequoia dying of old age. Sequoias balance on a broad root system. Most fallen ones have simply tipped over when erosion washed the soil from one side.

The General Sherman is too big to bore and get a growth ring count, but it is estimated at 3,700 years of age. Think of that as you gaze up into the gnarled limbs and at the snag top battered by the centuries. This was a mature tree when Christ was born. It was standing when Egypt's civilization flowered. In these trees you can witness a living time link with most of human history.

And a link with earth's history, too, for the sequoia trees date from the age of dinosaurs more than a hundred million years ago. They survived the Ice Age in sheltered basins in the mountains, just as their cousins did on the mild shores of California and Oregon and as another recently discovered relative, the dawn redwood, survived in China.

When you see the thousands of young sequoias growing in the park you may, in a sense, be looking thousands of years into the future. Given continued protection, many will still be living long after our present-day civilization is ancient history.

Young sequoias have a tough start in life. Relatively few seeds sprout (giant sequoias do not sprout from burls like the coast redwoods) and those that do demand proper soil and moisture. But they grow moderately fast.

Sequoia wood is remarkably resistant to rot and blight and, when mature, the tree trunks are "fireproofed" by their spongy bark that is sometimes two feet thick. But even if repeated fires pierce this armor and burn them out, so long as a ribbon of sapwood remains they live on, healing their wounds.

Notice this particularly in the blackened hulk of the Keyhole Tree, the Room Tree, hollowed by fire, the lightning-smashed Stricken Tree and many other scarred and wounded oldsters as you walk in the Giant Forest. And do walk. As in all parks, the man who walks here enjoys rewards far greater than one who stays by his car. Don't overdo it at first by trying to climb a mountain, for you are already at a high altitude.

The trails through Giant Forest are easy and beautiful, however, especially in the late afternoon when the long light reddens the sequoia trunks and casts graceful shadows.

The Congress Group walk takes you by the Senate and House, two of the largest and handsomest groups of giants, and by the Cloister and Founders' Group. Also nearby are the President, Washington, Lincoln and Chief Sequoyah trees, all nearly as big as the Sherman. The Chief Sequoyah honors the Cherokee leader who devised the first Indian alphabet. Botanist Stephan Endlicher admired the Indian linguist and named the sequoia genus for him, changing the spelling to conform with Latin.

The trails through Giant Forest will also take you past beautiful little meadows filled with wildflowers. In June they will be rosy with Sierra shooting stars; later, white with Queen Anne's lace and yellow with senecio. You may come across California mule deer browsing.

In one meadow, the hollow trunk of a huge fallen sequoia has been made into a cabin. Here Hale Tharp and his family spent summer weeks when he grazed stock in the meadows before the park was established in 1890. Here also he entertained John Muir, the great writer-naturalist who was hiking in his beloved Sierras with only his mule Brownie as company. Muir, who named the Giant Forest, called Tharp's log a "noble den . . . likely to outlast the most durable stone castle, and commanding views of garden and grove grander far than the richest king ever enjoyed." Alarmed at the destruction of many sequoia stands by lumbering operations, he joined those whose efforts led to protection of the trees.

Conservationist John Muir said, "No doubt these trees (sequoias) would make good lumber after passing through a saw mill, as George Washington after passing through the hands of a French chef would have made good food."

Muir's spirit and love of the wilderness lives on in the thousands of visitors who go adventuring into the great jagged mountains which tower beyond the sequoias. The original park reserve was nearly doubled in size in 1923 and now includes, along with Kings Canyon Park, a chunk of wild Sierra country the size of Rhode Island. The granite peaks, carved by glaciers and jeweled with emerald meadows and sapphire tarns, culminate in Mount Whitney, 14,495 feet in elevation, the highest mountain in the contiguous United States.

Snow-patched peaks with near-vertical precipices mark back country skyline of 14,500-foot Sierra summits.

"What a way to die!" exulted an older but eager outdoorsman when warned by a doctor not to attempt to climb the peak. Though strenuous, the hike up Whitney is made by many each year, most of whom approach from the east side of the Sierra, from Owens Valley. The Sierra Nevada rises abruptly here, and nine passes afford a quick approach to the heart of the mountain fastness of Sequoia and Kings Canyon National Parks.

Wrangler leads saddle horses and pack mule across a lingering snow field. The joint parks are big enough to provide pack trip parties with expeditions of many days, and offer wilderness experience at its very best.

Sequoia and Kings Canyon National Parks

Central California. Area: 1,314 sq. mi.
Season: year round. Main activities June-Sept.
Climate: warm days, cool nights. Elev. 6,000-14,000 ft.
Accommodations: lodges, tent chalets, cabins, trailer sites.
Services: many trails, fishing, museum.
State highways 180, 65, 198 lead to park.

Ferguson Canyon, a day's walk from the road, is a glaciated valley, with a broad, lush meadow at bottom.

Kings Canyon is Sequoia's neighbor to the north, and both parks are administered by the same National Park Service staff. Kings Canyon, established in 1940, includes the former General Grant National Park, which was set aside in 1890 to preserve the beautiful Grant Grove of sequoia trees.

The outstanding tree there, the General Grant, is second in size only to the Sherman, and many think the symmetrical giant even more impressive.

The General Grant Tree is widely known as the Nation's Christmas Tree, and Yuletide observances are held by it each year. Moreover, the Congress has named the General Grant a National Shrine honoring America's war dead.

The Grant Grove, reached most directly from Fresno, has many majestic giants, such as the California Tree, the General Lee, and the Fallen Monarch, whose hollow trunk was once used as a stable. But it is wilderness, stupendous wilderness, that is the chief characteristic of Kings Canyon National Park.

Take the canyon itself, for instance, where you can drive down to a camping area at Cedar Grove in the canyon bottom. The canyon of the Kings River is one of the deepest in North America: nearly 8,000 feet, in places, from mountaintop to riverbed.

The country beyond is equally grand, and through the heart of it, winds the John Muir Trail. This is the hikers' highway, running north through the Sierras for more than 200 miles, from Mount Whitney to Yosemite National Park.

The trail enters Kings Canyon National Park near Evolution Valley, mounts 11,000-foot Muir Pass and plunges into LeConte Canyon. It climbs Mather Pass, named for Stephen T. Mather, founder and first director of the National Park Service, passes Sixty-Lake Basin and crosses three more passes before entering the equally spectacular back country of Sequoia Park.

To this huge wilderness come lone backpackers, couples, and family groups; scout troops, college students, and outing clubs. They come in pack trains, with burros, and with knapsacks. Some fish for golden trout in the lakes and streams. Others break out climbing ropes to scale the cliffs. But most come to experience a primeval grandeur and beauty, and a close kinship with rock and meadow, water, flowers, and the bright, close stars.

With Muir, they agree that "In God's wildness lies the hope of the world—the great fresh, unblighted, unredeemed wilderness. The galling harness of civilization drops off, and the wounds heal ere we are aware." They too believe that "there is a love of wild nature in everybody, an ancient mother-love ever showing itself whether recognized or no, and however covered by cares and duties."

John Muir, the bearded wanderer whose science proved that glaciers carved these mountains and whose writings and influence helped to create at least six major parks and monuments and many wilderness areas, loved the Sierra with lyric understanding. As he walked it fearlessly alone, living on bread and tea, the wilderness was both a laboratory for research and a church for worship. "To get these glorious works of God into yourself—that's the thing," he once said.

"Climb the mountains and get their good tidings."

Rae Lake is one of hundreds in the back country. It lies on John Muir Trail, below 12,000-foot Glen Pass.

III · PLATEAU COUNTRY

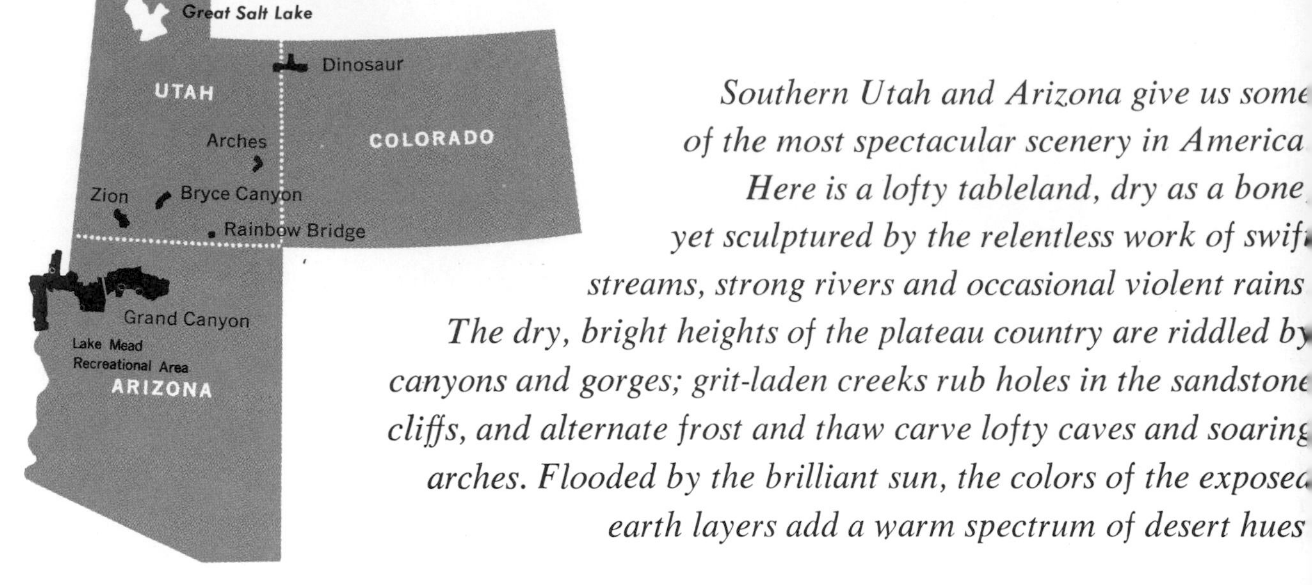

Southern Utah and Arizona give us some of the most spectacular scenery in America. Here is a lofty tableland, dry as a bone, yet sculptured by the relentless work of swift streams, strong rivers and occasional violent rains. The dry, bright heights of the plateau country are riddled by canyons and gorges; grit-laden creeks rub holes in the sandstone cliffs, and alternate frost and thaw carve lofty caves and soaring arches. Flooded by the brilliant sun, the colors of the exposed earth layers add a warm spectrum of desert hues.

Grand Canyon National Park ARIZONA

Theodore Roosevelt once said the Grand Canyon is something every American ought to see. Millions have taken his advice; thousands of cars climb to the two rims every summer day and tens of thousands of visitors stand and stare at a true wonder of the world.

Don't picture Grand Canyon as simply a deep, wide gorge in northern Arizona. Its walls do not drop straight to the Colorado River, then rise on the other side. Instead, this is an immense and complex badland—an example of erosion on a stupendous scale.

About 7,000,000 years ago there began a gradual uplifting of the land through which the Colorado flowed at little more than sea level. The river picked up speed. It scoured into the earth's surface, maintaining its level as the land rose around it. At that stretch of river that now forms Grand Canyon the land domed slightly. But the current held to its path, grinding its way through the hump. Its tributaries, too, chewed through the rising surface of the dome. Centuries of rain and snow, of seepage working into rock crevices then freezing and expanding, carved and shaped the rock formations that rise between the water-scoured cuts.

The process is still going on. The river is still chiseling its bed and the canyon is still being widened. Rocks, sand, and boulders, washed downstream serve as its abrasive tools. Grand Canyon, the river's handiwork, is a nether world of chasms and side canyons, of tenuous fins and sculptured buttes—the so-called "temples" like Zoroaster, Brahma, Buddha, Deva, Thor, Vishnu, and many others named for deities. It stretches 217 miles, averages 10 miles in width and is about a mile deep.

The casual visitor, rolling west on U.S. 66, makes a detour to the north at Flagstaff, Arizona, then follows the signs to the South Rim of Grand Canyon. He parks at Grand Canyon Village—a complete resort with a railroad station, general store, three fine hotels and a motel, a post office and a hospital—and walks a little way along East or West Rim trails. He looks out at this majestic landscape constantly changing color as the sun progresses. He is aware of silence, for this vast panorama swallows sound. He spends an hour

PRECEDING PAGE: *One mile deep, 13 miles wide, Grand Canyon bares sediments a billion and a half years old.*

buys a post card in a hotel lobby, and drives off with the almost uneasy knowledge that he has touched something awesome.

What such tourists see is a fraction of what Grand Canyon National Park offers. With more care and expenditure a man can get down into the canyon, stay there for a couple of days, understand it, and return to the atomic age with a humbling concept of the forces that built the world. For Grand Canyon's walls display the early geological history of the earth—the Pre-Cambrian and Paleozoic eras. The two later eras, Mesozoic and Cenozoic, have eroded away from the rims, but are represented at Zion Canyon and Bryce Canyon, respectively. If there were a way of putting these neighboring three national parks on top of each other, geologists would have a complete and continuous history of the earth.

Hiking down the trail can be a stimulating trip, but unless you are tough and conditioned to climbing in blistering heat, muleback is your method of transportation down into the canyon. Reserve your mule well ahead of time—also a cabin at Phantom Ranch, on the canyon floor. As you start switchbacking down Bright Angel Trail your hair will rise as your mule leans far out over the abyss at every turn. But Grand Canyon's mules are true professionals. Trust them, and do as your guide tells you.

You descend past grayish limestone walls, once marine sediments, the floor of an ancient sea. Then your trail passes yellowish sandstone, the sand dunes of an earlier age. The rock continues to change texture and color as you pass from stratum to stratum, always moving back in time. At the Redwall, where the trail swings into another series of switchbacks known as Jacob's Ladder, you are passing more sea deposits holding fossil shells. By the time you have reached the greenish rock known as Bright Angel Shale, your mule has carried you back in time to the earliest indication of the Paleozoic Era where trilobites, primitive crab-like animals, are fossilized. You have dropped some 3,000 feet from the South Rim—and you have gone back hundreds of millions of years.

After lunch on the Tonto Plateau you ride down into the Inner Gorge. This is the artery of Grand Canyon—a steep-walled cut more than 1,000 feet deep where the Colorado River rushes. You find the rock walls getting darker as you descend. These are Pre-Cambrian layers. Those at the lower level, the early Pre-Cambrian, were formed nearly two billion years ago. They contain no fossils to give an indication of life on earth. They lie here, uncovered by the grinding

The Colorado River, seen from the rim, seems to be a thin ribbon. Actually it is a deep and powerful river.

river, as reminders of a youthful earth whose sands and mud were squeezed by tremendous pressures into solid schist, which was then intruded by fingers of molten stone, which slowly cooled into pink granite.

A narrow suspension bridge crosses the Colorado at the bottom of the canyon. Here you can look down at the red, roaring stream, funneled into a millrace. It carries half a million tons of soil each day past where you stand—and that's not counting boulders.

Your eleven-mile trip from South Rim ends at Phantom Ranch, a welcome oasis for the tenderfoot. It even boasts a swimming pool—and a climate that is warm enough to go with it though it may be quite chilly up on the rims.

Your mule train returns to South Rim next morning on the Kaibab Trail. But if you have hiked instead of ridden, you may have planned a cross-canyon trip. You follow the relatively straight Bright Angel Canyon. You pass Ribbon Falls and Roaring Springs and wind up the canyon's north face to Bright Angel Point. Here you are about 1,200 feet higher than the South Rim, some 10 air miles away, and more than 200 miles distant by highway.

North Rim scenery is that of the wild Kaibab Plateau—mountain meadows and virgin evergreens. Grand Canyon Lodge, far out on the point, looks down into the canyon. Nearby are other lodges and ample camping space.

A family could spend its entire vacation in 1,100-square-mile Grand Canyon National Park and not repeat the trips and adventures that it offers. With special arrangements, tourists can visit the Havasupai Indian Reservation, a remote and beautiful pocket of rich bottomland in Havasu Canyon. Make reservations with Havas Development Enterprise, Supai, Arizona. Yo must cook your own food while in the reservatior

Or you may wish to visit adjoining Grand Canyon National Monument, an undeveloped wildeness that offers, at Toroweap Point, the most spec

Grand Canyon National Park

N Arizona. Area: 1,052 sq. mi.

Season: south rim year round, north rim May 15-Oct. 15.

Climate: s. rim warm days, cool nights; elev. 6,900 ft. n. rim cooler; elev. 8,900 ft. Canyon floor hot.

Accommodations: lodges, campgrounds, trailer pks.

Services: hosp., restaurants, stores, gar., serv. in park.

State highway 64, from US 89 or 66; Santa Fe Ry lead to park.

tacular view of the Colorado River—3,000 feet straight down. You reach it from the North Rim, going off at Fredonia, Arizona on a desert road.

Grand Canyon is big enough and rugged enough to be dangerous. Pay attention to Park Service rules and never hesitate to ask the advice of a ranger about any trip you may wish to make. If you allow a few days for your muscles to harden you will enjoy all the more this splendid park.

Bright Angel Trail threads down to the river. Hikers allow one day each way. Mule riders return same day.

Bryce Canyon National Park UTAH

Ebenezer Bryce, the Mormon rancher who left Bryce Canyon its name, said it was "a hell of a place to lose a cow." The Paiute Indians called it "red rocks standing like men in a bowl-shaped canyon." A tourist once described it as "a pink-and-white birthday cake, candles and all."

Some of the most exquisitely colored rocks of the earth's crust, cut and shaped into weird and wonderful forms, are to be found in Utah's Bryce Canyon National Park. Bryce is the youngest of a famous trio of southwestern canyons – Grand Canyon is the senior, Zion Canyon ranks second in age. In one-two-three order, all were formed by erosion of a huge plateau that has been rising steadily for the last 12 million years. But whereas Grand Canyon was gouged out by the mighty Colorado river itself, and Zion by the swift Virgin River, Bryce is being whittled out of new, tabletop rocks by tiny rivulets, at the geologically greedy rate of one foot every 50 years.

Actually, Bryce is not a canyon at all but a large, horseshoe-shaped bowl cut out of the 8,000-foot-high Paunaugunt Plateau. Entering the park, you find the information center, lodge, inn and campgrounds set alongside a road that runs for 18 miles on the lip of this bowl. Just stop at one of the parking places alongside this rim road, say at Sunset Point, and you see the big amphitheater at your feet (and 80 miles of Utah mountains rolling majestically away in the background).

The colors are a feast for the eyes – corals, oranges, roses, every shade from white to Cordovan brown. The gorgeous hues of Bryce change with the sunlight but basically come from metal in the park's limestones and sandstones. What you see are traces of manganese and iron in different stages of oxydization–the rust of the rocks.

From the rim, easy trails lead down to a close view of Bryce's fantastic spires and columns. The

Bryce Canyon National Park

SW Utah. Area: 56 sq. mi.

Season: visitor center year round, Rainbow Pt. Rd. April-Dec.

Climate: warm, dry, nights cold. Elev. 8,000-9,100 ft.

Accommodations: lodge, campgrounds, trailer site.

Services: restaurant, stores, gar., hosp., serv. in park.

US highway 89, state highway 12 lead to park.

Wall of Windows stretches above a riding party. Colors are from metallic oxides, range from red to white.

Navajo Loop, the one trail on which a ranger guide is provided, drops in a series of hairpin turns down a 35-degree slope through Wall Street, a chasm so narrow and shadowed that it suggests Manhattan's skyscraper-edged canyons. Miles of good walking and horseback trails thread the weird formations of Queen's Garden, Peekaboo Canyon, and other stone wonderlands. You can find an 80-foot natural bridge, a towering rock that looks (they say) like Queen Victoria, and hatpin-like pinnacles crowned by fat boulders.

Zion National Park UTAH

Many travelers find Zion National Park a big surprise. Heading north from Grand Canyon, or south from Bryce Canyon, they rather expect to find it an anticlimax. Instead, they find Zion Canyon a giant to match its famous neighbors.

Zion's color is red—red in let's say thirty-five varieties. Driving east from Hurricane, Utah, you see red, crimson red, when you approach the park's south entrance and sight the great shoulder of West Temple on your left. You see red, vermilion red, when you thread your way up the shadowy canyon floor to glimpse Angels Landing jutting 2,000 feet straight above you. And you see red, a kind of white red, when you leave your car near West Rim Trail, and look across the plunging gorge at the towering dome called the Great White Throne. Finally you realize that the rocks take their various tints from sunlight and shifting shadows, and the red of Zion seems like every color you ever saw.

The red of Zion is sandstone, stained by iron and manganese oxides carried in solution by water, and deposited during the slow filtering of millions of years when this part of the Southwest lay beneath ancient seas. In the three-part geological history of the Southwest, Zion Canyon belongs in the middle, right between ancient history as told in the Grand Canyon and modern history as shown in Bryce. Start reading this wonderful history in stone at the bottom of mile-deep Grand Canyon, climb upwards with the ages, past a billion years of time, and as you step onto the rim you will find it cut off suddenly at your feet, a story broken off with 150,000,000 years left to tell. The sandstones and shales that once lay above that level have been planed right away from the Grand Canyon landscape. To find them, you need only travel north to Zion. As the crow flies, it is only 60 miles, but by car it is a 230-mile swing from Grand Canyon Village on the South Rim. There are the missing pages, and since these particular rock-pages are so soft and porous, they are carved and shaped into all sorts of fantastic forms.

This is how it happened. About 13 million years ago, when the Zion country was low and level, the entire Southwest began slowly to rear up

The view from a high lookout point, Angel's Landing, 2,000 feet above the park road and the Virgin River.

Walter's Wiggles, "where a horse goes two ways at the same time," scales a steep cliff up to Angel's Landing.

—it may still be rearing up. In the vast uplift, the land mass broke into great blocks, cracking along lines in the rock called faults. The uplift turned the lazy Virgin River, running through Zion park, into a racing torrent. With its tributaries, the Virgin's swift waters cut deep along the fault lines, grinding up and carrying away huge quantities of rock. Finally a mile-deep layer that had once been desert dunes was laid bare—the Navajo sandstone you now see in Zion park.

Rain, frost and tree roots eat steadily at the soft rock. The river falls steeply, nine times as steeply as the Colorado River in Grand Canyon. And Zion's sandstone happens to be even-textured, without sandwiched-in layers of different hardness. The rock weakens first at the bottom, causing big vertical slabs to fall. It is this oddity that makes Zion Canyon's sheer walls, almost 2,500 feet straight up along the eight miles of road from the park gate to the road's end at the little oasis called the Temple of Sinawava.

Of all Zion's magnificent trails, the most popular is the footpath that starts at the road's end at the Temple of Sinawava, and leads on for a mile to the Narrows. Here the canyon becomes a mere slit in the rocks and here, in the cool, green twilight, you can see the summer-blooming Zion moonflower, whose trumpet-shaped blossoms open fully only at dusk. Or, taking your lunch, you can push off from the parking lot at Weeping Rock for an all-day hike or horseback trip up the East Rim Trail, where you may see a bobcat. A more strenuous trail, starting at the Grotto campground, follows a track chipped out of the vertical wall of

Weary hikers peer over a cliff twice as high as the Empire State Building. Angel's Landing in background.

the Canyon's West Rim and leads past Great West Canyon toward the magnificent back country added to the park when Zion National Monument was joined to it in 1956.

Zion has two large campgrounds in the canyon, an inn and Zion Lodge, which is famous as a spot for viewing Zion Canyon by moonlight. Sunrise and sunset are also daily dramas in Zion's deep, narrow, vertically walled chasm: dusk falls fast when the sun disappears over the sheer palisade of the 6,723-foot-high Mountain of the Sun.

Even if you enter and leave the canyon by the park's south gate, you should make a special effort to take the 11-mile drive along the highway leading from the canyon to the park's east entrance. This road, known as the Zion-Mt. Carmel highway, belongs with Yosemite's Tioga Pass and Glacier's Logan Pass among the great mountain roads of the United States. From the Virgin River bridge it climbs in six sharp switchbacks to a mile-long tunnel through the Zion Canyon wall. The tunnel has six openings, all of which reveal dazzling views, one disclosing the sandstone rainbow of Zion's Great Arch. Incidentally, when the tunnel was dug these galleries were opened first and the debris thrown in the creekbed below. It is a measure of water's swift work that within months a few cloudbursts had washed most of the debris away downstream and right out of the park. Beyond the tunnel, the Zion-Mt. Carmel highway leads past one example of oddly faulted and bizarrely eroded sandstone after another. The most spectacular is Checkerboard Mesa, a 6,670-foot-high mountain whose sandstone is cut horizontally by the lines of ancient desert windrows and vertically along cracks created by later uplifts.

Of all our national parks, Zion is the one most closely associated with Mormon history. It was first visited by the fur-trapper Jedediah Smith, who named the Virgin River after one of his comrades in the early 19th century. But Apostle Brigham Young of the Latter-day Saints soon after led his wagon train into Utah and said: "This is the place." The Mormons quickly spread southward from Salt Lake. As diligent as they were de vout, they soon began irrigating and tilling land along the Virgin River. It was the Mormons, stirre by the valley's "towering temples of stone," wh first called the place Zion, which means "the heav enly city of God." St. George, Orderville anc Springdale are some of the historic Mormon set tlements to look for along your road to Zion.

Zion National Park

SW Utah. Area: 233 sq. mi.
Season: year round.
Climate: summer days hot, nights cool.
Accommodations: lodge, inn, camps, trailer sites.
Services: restaurant, stores, garages, serv. in park.
US highway 89 or 91 to Utah 15. Bus connections.

Arches National Monument

UTAH

During the past billion or so years the cooling earth has shrunk and its crust has cracked and kinked in countless ways. Seas have formed, then vanished, leaving sediments to harden into sandstone, to crack, and to fold.

A thick layer of sandstone in southeastern Utah forms the famous red rock country, a fantastic land of gorges, buttes, and pinnacles. Arches National Monument preserves 53 square miles of this country where the earth's shifting has split the sandstone into regular rows, like corduroy. Over the years some of these rows crumbled and washed away. But others still stand in orderly array, their rainwashed cracks now widened and interconnected to form a maze of passageways, dimly lit by pink reflections from the shining walls.

Some rows, or fins, stand alone in a thousand grotesque shapes. Most remarkable are those whose lower sections were undercut and pierced by the splitting and flaking effects of frost and water. So far, 88 of these arches and windows have been found.

The headquarters of Arches National Monument lies on U.S. 160, five miles north of Moab. From there a good road leads to areas of interest and trails strike out to the choicest features. The trail to Delicate Arch is itself a spectacular thing. Cut right into the side of a plummeting cliff, it leads to one of the loneliest and most beautiful sights in the world.

Arches National Monument

SE Utah. Area: 53 sq. mi.
Season: year round.
Climate: days hot, nights cool.
Accommodations: none. 7-day limit for campers.

The Fiery Furnace is a maze of red-walled passageways. Here, two hikers pause beside a pure pool below a spillway.

Delicate Arch stands on the rim of a tall promontory.

Dinosaur National Monument COLORADO UTAH

The richest quarry of dinosaur bones in the world is an upturned ledge of rock in the dry northeast corner of Utah. Since 1909 scientists have dug out two dozen complete skeletons from this jam-packed natural storehouse, along with parts of 300 other monsters. Yet today the skeletons of dozens more lie still embedded in the rock. In a huge modern building that covers the site paleontologists daily chip at the entombing stone. Visitors are welcome to watch them at work, and to view the bones as they lie in place—the only museum of its kind in the world. Park Service naturalists answer questions, and side exhibits tell the story of these long-gone beasts.

The word "dinosaur" comes from the Greek *deinos* (meaning terrible) and *sauros* (lizard). Whether these lizards were all terrible is doubtful, but some of them certainly were huge. *Brontosaurus* stretched 70 feet long and weighed more than 34 tons. *Stegosaurus* was about as big as an elephant. He had a double row of huge bony plates running down his back, and a powerful tail tipped with four great spikes. But he was unbelievably stupid: his brain was no bigger than a kitten's. *Allosaurus* was a flesh eater. Tall as a giraffe, he stood on powerful hind legs and tore at his food with jagged, shark-like teeth. Still others stood no taller than a turkey.

Stupid as they were (one pound of brain served 30 tons of weight whereas an elephant has a nine-pound brain for his four-ton body) dinosaurs were incredibly successful. They first appeared 200 million years ago and for 140 million years thereafter were the dominant form of life on earth. No human ever saw a live dinosaur. After the last one died 60 million years ago there was a gap of 59½ million years before man as we know him appeared. The 500,000 years that human beings have lived on the earth is a mere moment in this colossal scale of time.

What killed the dinosaurs? Nobody knows for sure. But scientists do know that when they lived,

World's richest dinosaur quarry is this rock face in the visitor center. Experts daily uncover more bones.

the now mountainous desert around Dinosaur National Monument was a flat marshland. Meandering streams, fed by increasing rainfall, threaded the area and became raging torrents. Volcanoes shot clouds of ash into the air. Whether floods or volcanoes or both killed the dinosaurs, we are not sure. Their carcasses nevertheless floated downstream and came to rest on a sand bar, there to be covered by more sands and ultimately to petrify. As the millions of years passed more sediments settled on top of the old until eventually some 5,000 feet of stone covered the ancient bones.

Then, ages later, forces within the earth heaved the rock strata up into mountains. Erosion removed the softer layers from the mountain tops and left their upturned edges exposed. Rain and frost wore down the tipped-up rock, and once again the long-buried skeletons came to light.

Today this storehouse of bones in the Quarry Visitor Center 7 miles north of Jensen, Utah, is the focal point of the national monument. A campground is located at Split Mountain Gorge nearby.

But fossils discovery is only half the story of Dinosaur Monument. Stretching eastward from the quarry lies a 328-square-mile area of rugged canyon country, added to the 80-acre quarry site in 1938. Though rainfall is scarce, water is the key to its beauty, for two spectacular, canyon-enclosed rivers join here. Castle Park, Island Park, Little Rainbow Park and the incomparable Echo Park are shady oases spotted along the river bottoms.

This is true wilderness. As yet no modern roads penetrate the area. Echo Park lies 37 miles, partly by dirt road, from U.S. 40. But the drive is worth it. Just below the junction of the Green and Yampa rivers, and facing Echo Park, stands Steamboat Rock, jutting up in the river like a colossal ship. Near here also is Harper's Corner, a high point overlooking the rugged canyon country. Few places in the national park system are so wildly beautiful, few campgrounds more remote than the one located here.

Below Steamboat Rock the Green cuts through Whirlpool Canyon, flows quietly by Island Park Ranch (also reachable by car, or better yet by jeep) and plunges into Split Mountain Canyon. After a rushing journey between red and cream-striped walls towering a half mile overhead, the river flows past the main campground, and peacefully enters Utah's broad Uinta Valley.

A rubber boat rides down the Green River.

An adventurous way to see Dinosaur is by float trip through the canyons. Though the rivers are swift the trip is safe enough in a large Navy rubber boat. Ordinary outboards, canoes, and rowboats definitely are not safe, for once you enter the canyons there is no way of walking back in case of a spill. Best boating time is May through July. Professional river boatmen take groups down the river by appointment. Trips last several days. Write the Superintendent, Artesia, Colorado for details.

Dinosaur has no hotel, restaurants, or stores. For supplies and accommodations, head for Vernal on U.S. 40, 13 miles west of the turn-off to Dinosaur Quarry Visitor Center at Jensen.

Dinosaur National Monument

N centr. Utah, N Colorado Area: 328 sq. mi.
Season: May-Sept.
Climate: hot days, cool evenings.
Accommodations: trailer grounds.
Services: visitor center, museum.
US 40, State 149 highways lead to park.

Rainbow Bridge National Monument UTAH ARIZONA

People have traveled great distances at staggering expense, gone hungry and thirsty, risked tumbling down cliffs and drowning in the turbid Colorado River in order to see Rainbow Bridge. Until recently it was one of the most inaccessible treasures of the national park system, tucked away in a wilderness of twisting red rock canyons near the Colorado-Utah line. But Glen Canyon Dam on the Colorado is forming a lake that will bring casual tourists close to this magnificent span of smooth, solid rock, the world's largest natural bridge.

Rainbow Bridge is big enough to fit over the Capitol at Washington. Yet it is swallowed by far taller canyon walls. And so perfect are its proportions that visitors don't appreciate its true size until they stand under it, craning up at its soaring arch, or venture out on top of it, with the canyon floor far, far below.

The bridge was formed by water finding its way through this red sandstone plateau. In a series of hairpin turns—meanders—the primeval stream gnawed its way around high spurs of rock. It washed against this spur, swung wide around it, then touched it again on the other side. Rocks and other debris, washed down by flash floods, struck the spur twice, very gradually wearing the stone away, and at last piercing it. The stream rushed through the breach, widening and rounding the hole. Wind-blown sand smoothed and polished the surface. Only nature, working for millions of years, could produce such a masterpiece.

Rainbow Bridge National Monument
Utah-Arizona border near Glen Canyon.
Accessible only by car or horse, from US 89.

The world's largest natural bridge, Rainbow spans 278 feet, and rises 309 feet above the creek that carved it.

Lake Mead is a boater's paradise. Water is warm and clear. Here, a desert sunset frames a water skier.

Lake Mead National Recreation Area NEVADA

An oasis in the most modern sense, Lake Mead National Recreation Area is a glorious reservoir of sparkling blue, crisscrossed by the wakes of water skiers, echoing to the shouts of swimmers. Cars jam its parking areas, boats whine past its shores, where thousands of people sunbathe.

National Recreation Area is a title given to places where the Park Service shares jurisdiction with other government agencies. Lake Mead was formed when the Bureau of Reclamation built huge Hoover Dam on the Colorado River. The bureau maintains the dam. The Park Service welcomes visitors.

The area includes two lakes: Mead, backed up by Hoover Dam, and Mohave, behind Davis Dam. Mead extends 115 miles, right up into Grand Canyon. Its northern branch backs into the Muddy and Virgin rivers. Lake Mohave is 67 miles long. The Recreation Area lies on the border of Arizona and Nevada and its eastern end adjoins Grand Canyon National Monument. When full, Lake Mead ranks among the largest artificial lakes anywhere—it is nearly 600 feet deep.

Eight developments offer access to the lakes with beaches, marinas, lodges, and campgrounds. Fishing is fine: largemouth bass grow big, and rainbows have been introduced in the upper reaches of Mohave, where the water is colder than the warmer temperature of the lakes.

Summer is hot here. The other seasons are fine for hiking and taking scenic drives, but check road and trail conditions first.

The Lake Mead area is easily reached from either Las Vegas, Nevada, or Kingman, Arizona.

Lake Mead National Recreation Area
S Nevada nr. Arizona border.

IV · THE SOUTHWEST

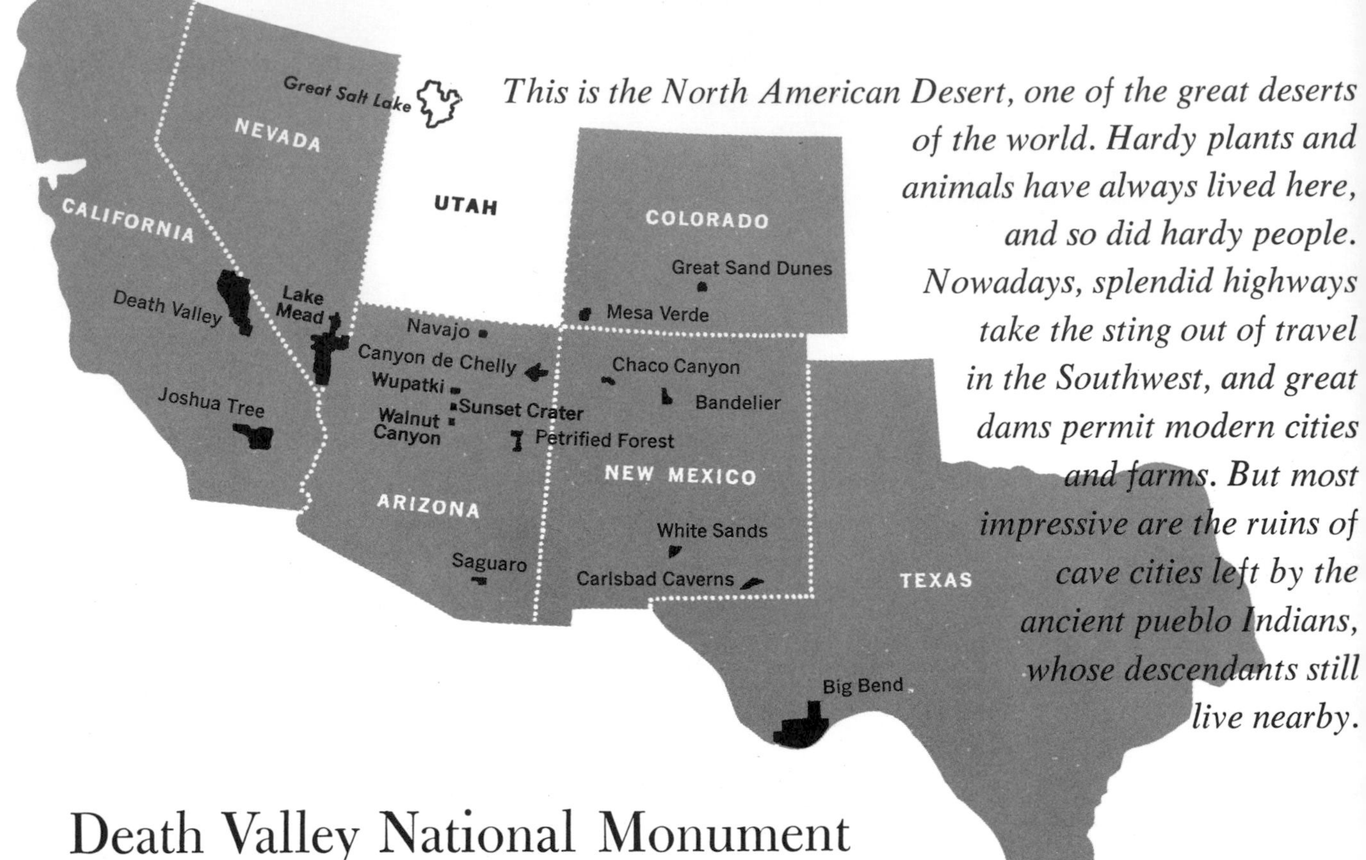

This is the North American Desert, one of the great deserts of the world. Hardy plants and animals have always lived here, and so did hardy people. Nowadays, splendid highways take the sting out of travel in the Southwest, and great dams permit modern cities and farms. But most impressive are the ruins of cave cities left by the ancient pueblo Indians, whose descendants still live nearby.

Death Valley National Monument

CALIFORNIA NEVADA

The name is repelling—and hardly fair. For though this 140-mile-long California valley, bordering Nevada, *looks* inhospitable—and certainly is in the scorching heat of summer—it blossoms with especially adaptable plants and bustles at night with the activities of desert animals from ground squirrel to kit fox. Tourists crowd Death Valley's privately run lodgings: Furnace Creek Inn and Ranch, Stove Pipe Wells Hotel, and Scotty's Castle. Cars hum up and down the highway that splits this nearly 2,000,000-acre national monument.

From Dante's View, about 28 miles south of monument headquarters, you can look across the valley and beyond the grim Panamint Range that forms its western wall to distant Mt. Whitney, California's highest point. And below you lies a long ribbon of flat desert floor, all of it below sea level, with one spot sinking 282 feet—the lowest in the Western Hemisphere. This salt-caked bottom land was once the bed of a 100-mile-long lake, formed in the moist days of the Ice Age. The uplift of the Sierras changed climate and cut off much rainfall. The lake evaporated and its concentrated salts dried, cracked into chunks, and heaved and tilted as crystals formed underneath. Years of erosion have left the jagged, 40-mile salt plain known as Devils Golf Course.

Another spectacle is the pile of sand dunes north of headquarters, and yet another is Ubehebe Crater at the monument's northern end. Best of all are the varying colors on the mountain walls, the peaks that turn crimson in the setting sun.

Death Valley was no fun for its first white visitors. They were a group of forty-niners who stumbled into this sun-baked trench, four to sixteen miles wide, while "short-cutting" to the gold

PRECEDING PAGE: *A great sunken trench, Death Valley is a hot, dry desert carved by rare torrential rains.*

fields. One party, the Jayhawkers, jettisoned most of their gear and got across and to their destination. The Bennett-Arcane party spent nearly a month here during the winter of 1849, scrabbling for water and slowly starving. When they finally struggled out, one member looked back, muttering, "Goodby, Death Valley."

Hence the name, though only one man actually died within the valley. Prospectors nosed around the bleak hills, built hell-roaring towns like Chloride City, Greenwater, and Skidoo, and moved away again. One settler gathered borax and began a booming industry, complete with 20-mule teams. One of Buffalo Bill's trick riders, Walter E. Scott, perpetrated an enormous hoax by pretending to have struck it immensely rich in Death Valley. He had, in fact, made friends with a playful millionaire who built a monstrous castle for him. Now Scotty's Castle is a hotel.

Death Valley National Monument is open throughout the year. During the summer, the Park Service recommends that you travel through the area before noon as the afternoons are often very uncomfortable. Some facilities close in summer, but Wildrose Station, Scotty's Castle and others remain open.

Death Valley National Monument

S California-Nevada. Area: 2,981 sq. mi.

Season: year round, most facilities Oct. 15-May 1.

Climate: hot days, cool evenings.

Accommodations: seasonal: inns, hotels, cabins, camping and trailer sites.

US highways 95, 91, 395 lead to park.

A pool of stagnant water reflects the soft pink and amethyst colors of distant mountains.

Carlsbad Caverns National Park NEW MEXICO

The National Park Service people are not given to talking like Hollywood producers, and when they use an adjective, it has real meaning. So when your guide tells you at the start of your tour that "You are entering the world's most spectacular caverns," believe him. There is nothing else like it under this earth.

If you were to go through all of its explored parts, you would be setting out on a hike of several miles through many great passages and rooms. You'd find very little cramped space. In fact, quite a few large buildings could be built in some of the caverns. And the greatest of the caves, called Big Room, is large enough to hold a cathedral. One of its arms has a stretch of 2,000 feet—more than a third of a mile. And where its ceiling is 232 feet up, you would agree that there is room for a good steeple.

But the eye-filling pleasures of the caverns are not just their spaces. It is also how they have been decorated over hundreds of thousands of years by the action of seeping water on minerals. These two aspects of the caverns, first the spaces and then their decorations, took an immense amount of time.

The formative period began about 250 million years ago. It started with the growth of a limestone reef in what was then a shallow sea. The reef, made out of the limey part of animals and algae, eventually piled up 2,000 feet thick.

Then about 60 million years ago the uplift of the rocky Mountains caused stresses on the earth's crust which cracked the reef. This permitted surrounding ground water to enter and begin dissolving away the reef to form Carlsbad Caverns. About one million years ago the uplift of the local Guadalupe Mountains raised the reef above the water table. The water drained away and air filled the spaces where it had been.

The decorative period then set in. Surface water seeping through decaying vegetation picked up carbon dioxide and filtered down through the fis-

Onyx draperies cascade from the lofty ceiling of New Mexico's Carlsbad Caverns, the world's largest cave.

sured rock. This mixture of water and carbonic gas is a solvent for limestone. And so long as the water contains the gas, the limestone stays dissolved. But as the water dripped from the roof o a cave, the gas escaped into the air. The limestone then was expelled from the water and crusted o the cave surface. Layer after layer it built up following the lines of the dribbling water, just a does an icicle. It was the ages-long leaking of thi "hard water" down into the caverns that caused the stalactites, the icicle-like hangings, and the stalagmites, the pile-up of many shapes upon the floors of the caverns.

The dripping solution eventually created a endless variety of forms upon the walls as well a upon the ceiling and floors.

Some of these forms have been given aptl fitting names—American Eagle, Whale's Mouth

Three Little Monkeys, Baby Hippo. There is also the Rock of Ages, Temple of the Sun, Hall of Giants and the Iceberg, a great rock-fall of about 200,000 tons – large even for a sea-borne berg.

The guided tour is about three miles long, along a paved and well-lighted path. It starts at the natural opening to the caverns in the foothills of the Guadalupe Mountains. When first noticed back in the 1880's, this opening was thought of as only a home for bats which still take refuge in one of the rooms, called Bat Cave. Bats numbering in the hundreds of thousands have been estimated to sleep by day in that room. For obvious reasons Bat Cave is not included in the guided tour.

Years ago the nearby ranchers seemed to take the attitude that one would have to be batty himself to bother about a hole in the ground that was home to such a horde of squeaking flyers. But in 1901 a young cowboy, James Larkin White, took a kerosene lantern and ventured into the opening to find out why the bats liked it so.

He had to scramble over rocks and rubble where there are now ramps and even an elevator to bring you back to the surface at the close of your tour. What he saw started his several years of explorations in the cave. It became the main interest of his life. The fame of the caverns grew slowly, and in 1923 it was proclaimed a national monument and Jim White soon became chief park ranger. Then Congress voted it a national park in 1930.

Although the public's attention centers on Carlsbad Caverns, there are about 30 other cave systems in the 77-square-mile park. But none are equal to Carlsbad in size or beauty.

The chief spectacles of Carlsbad Caverns are pretty far underground. The 4-hour guided tour takes you down winding ramps about 830 feet to reach the first of the scenic chambers, the Green Lake Room, named after its pond. Then there is the King's Palace, the most intricately decorated. The Queen's chamber and the Papoose Room follow, and their names describe them. There are other fascinating sights, but the next item of major interest would be a delight for the eyes anywhere after a two-hour walk in the 56-degree air: the lunchroom where the tour takes a halt.

The tour's second part is a mile-and-a-quarter walk around the edges of the Big Room, the world's largest underground chamber – a grand canyon underground, almost. If the whole tour seems too strenuous, you can go down by elevator and join a walking tour after their lunch break. Then you return to the elevator close by the lunchroom and ride up about 754 feet to the surface and the three-story observation tower. Here you may look out on the rolling New Mexico desert that is roof to the caverns.

From that tower, you can see the approximate surface points of your underground tour. And the distances between the points will give you added awareness of the great reaches of the caverns.

From the tower you also may see some of the hundreds of mule deer which roam the cavern area. They and the bats are the area's important animals. For zoologists, amateur and professional, the bats are of even more interest than the caves.

Mostly, they are free-tailed bats, with a foot-long wingspread. They fly out at dusk at the rate of about 100 a second. And it may take as long as 4 hours for all of them to go. Each summer evening a park naturalist gives a talk on the bats.

The caverns are open all year. To reach them, you may come through Carlsbad, New Mexico, 27 miles to the northeast, or through El Paso, 170 miles to the west. Driving directions may be had from almost anyone in either place.

You will not be allowed to camp in the park, nor may you light a fire. And if you bring your own food, you will have to eat in a designated area. Adjoining the visitor center is a restaurant, a curio shop, a nursery where you may leave small children, and a kennel where you may leave even a large dog, while you go down to this most elaborate cellar in the earth.

Carlsbad Caverns National Park

SE New Mexico. Area: 77 sq. mi.

Season: year round.

Weather: 100° + in summer, ± 0° in winter. Cave 56°, elev. 4,350 ft.

Accommodations: hotels, motels, trailer sites.

Services: restaurant, curio shops, garage, car rental, hosp., church 27 mi. NE of caverns.

US highways 62, 180, 285, air, rail and coaches lead to park.

Big Bend National Park TEXAS

This is no place for sissies. Part mountain, part desert, and part coyote and rattlesnake, Texas' enormous national park, wedged in the great bend of the Rio Grande, is a challenge even for the tough Texans who visit it.

It's been said that here every plant "either sticks, stings, or stinks," but that doesn't keep them from being beautiful. Desert flowers bloom in amazing variety and color from spring right through to fall. In summer the temperature frequently soars above 100° in the flat country. But a comfortable 85° is normal in the Basin of the Chisos Mountains where you may make your headquarters. Nights there are cool and rain is scarce. Oldtimers say that a five-inch rain in Big Bend means a few drops five inches apart. But sometimes sudden squalls can turn dusty arroyos into foaming cataracts. Then a half hour later it is dry again. A drizzle is a rare thing.

Big Bend is a spectacular place. But Texans will try to exaggerate anything and a lot of tall tales have come out of this country. Like Pecos Bill, for instance, who saddled a tornado but got "throwed" when it rained out from under him.

Because the park is so vast, many visitors plan to stay at least three or four days. Anything less would amount to a non-stop round trip.

Strawberry cactus has lovely blossoms and edible fruit.

There are two entrances to the park. Northernmost is through Persimmon Gap via U.S. 385. This follows the old Comanche Trail, a raiding route to Mexico for painted warriors of 100 years ago. The other entrance is at Maverick Mountain, on state route 118, 80 miles south of Alpine. The two roads converge at Panther Junction, site of park headquarters. Here you're in the shadow of the Chisos Mountains, once a refuge for badmen and Indians, now a haven for vacationers.

Drive up Green Gulch and through Panther Pass to enter The Basin, a great saucerlike depression in the heart of the Chisos. Only here has the 20th century invaded the park with cottages, campgrounds, a grocery store, and telephone. Here you can enjoy evening campfire talks by the park naturalist and rangers, eat chow at the Chuck Wagon dining hall, and take horseback trips to high ridges.

The Chisos are ragged, toothy mountains without symmetry. At 7,500 feet they can hardly be said to "tower," but that they exist at all is a wonder. Eons ago Big Bend was nothing but a vast sea. Silt and mineral deposits eventually formed sedimentary layers which later rose above the sea and folded into mountains. The sea returned and more sedimentary rock, including sea shells and marine fossils, built up. Again the sea receded. Forests and bogs took over, and dinosaurs moved in.

Then the earth strata uplifted again, molten lava squeezed up through fissures and hardened, eruptions spewed out volcanic dust and cinders. In time, wind and water filed smooth some of the edges and sharpened others. What resulted was awesome beauty and ruggedness: flattened mesas, pointed mountains, cathedral-like monuments of stone, and deep winding canyons.

"Nowhere else have I found such a wildly weird country," wrote William Ferguson, U.S. Treasury agent who came to Big Bend in 1895. "Never

The Rio Grande emerges meekly from Santa Elena Canyon. Cliff on left is in Mexico, the right one, in U.S.

Stillwell Crossing bridges the Rio Grande to Mexico a few miles below the eastern boundary of the park.

have I beheld such a display of glory as falls at sunset on the bald head of the Chisos Mountains," he said.

The Chisos are a photographer's paradise. Red and orange highlights glimmer against deep purple shadows at sunrise and evening. From the South Rim you can look into Mexico and "see the day after tomorrow." Or you can aim your lens at the variegated desert spangled with yucca and strawberry cactus.

A roadrunner can fly very well; he runs because he prefers to. His favorite food is snakes, even rattlers.

At the southern edge, bordering Mexico for 107 miles, the Rio Grande drifts through sandy flats and cuts through deep gorges. Its general course is a sweeping curve—the Big Bend. Sometimes it is not much of a river. You can walk across in most places during low water.

In general the water flows peaceably, but there are sections that challenge even expert boatmen. Anyone who wants to make a float trip down the Rio Grande should first write the Park superintendent.

At the western edge of Big Bend is Santa Elena Canyon, whose walls are 1,200 feet high and in most places rise vertically right out of the river. Here, lunker catfish prowl the deep holes. Near Terlingua Creek picnickers and hikers can stand at water's edge and wet a line while they absorb the immensity of the canyon.

At the eastern edge of the park is 25-mile-long

Boquillas Canyon, longest of Big Bend's gorges. Mexican bandits crossed near here in 1916 and were chased back into Mexico by U. S. Cavalry troops. But Boquillas is threatened today by nothing fiercer than wide-eyed tourists. At night, winking lights in Mexican adobes can be seen clustered across the river.

In general Big Bend is nearly as deserted as when Cabeza de Vaca, a lost Spanish soldier making his way back to Mexico, stumbled through this country in 1535. Except in the lowlands where mule deer and pronghorns browse among mesquite and cottonwoods, there is scarcely enough to eat and drink even for such intent foragers as the peccary or ringtail. These in turn make hard-won meals for the mountain lion and kit fox.

Birds, from cactus wren to roadrunner, find the park a spacious refuge. Big Bend is the only known nesting place in the U. S. for the rare Colima warbler.

Big Bend is so wild—parts of it are yet to be explored—that rangers insist that you stick to the trails. Remember, this is desert. It is magnificent but water is scarce. A greenhorn who gets lost in its thousand square miles could die of thirst before he's found. Always pack a canteen when hiking. Carry water in your car. Wood is also scarce. If you intend to stay at one of the two campgrounds bring your own makings or a gasoline stove.

Jeans, thick-soled shoes or boots, and a broad-brimmed hat are essentials. A first-aid kit with tweezers will come in handy if you get vaccinated by a cactus spine, or stung by a scorpion. But don't let these hazards scare you. The wildlife stays holed up during the day, and in any event all animals, whether furry or scaly, will do their best to avoid you. Big Bend in all likelihood is safer than downtown Dallas on a Saturday night.

Big Bend National Park

SW Texas. Area: 708,000 acres.

Season: year round.

Climate: very hot in flat country, cooler near mountains.

Accommodations: campgrounds, trailer sites.

Park is 79 mi. S. of Marathon, Tex., on US 385.

An ocotillo waves its spindly branches in front of the Chisos Mountains, near the middle of the park.

Huge dune dwarfs a man walking its face. Climbing the face of a dune is exhausting, but sliding down is fun.

Great Sand Dunes National Monument COLORADO

As you drive east from Mosca, Colorado, across the San Luis Valley you notice these distant sand hills close under the steep wall of the Sangre de Cristo Mountains. You aim for the dunes at 60 miles an hour, yet they seem to get no nearer. In this clear, clean land objects 20 miles distant sometime look as if they were only two.

When at last you reach Great Sand Dunes you find them well worth the wait. Sand from the San Luis Valley, an ancient lake bed, is whirled off by the prevailing southwest wind, then dropped as air rises to clear the Sangre de Cristos. So the dunes are built in the same way as blowing snow forms drifts. And like snowdrifts they shift position and change shape. They rise to knife-edge ridges, are hollowed into craters, and rounded into whalebacks. Here in this 57-square-mile national monument are some of the tallest dunes in the world: about 800 feet high.

Medano Creek borders the dunes and fights a losing battle with them. Relentlessly, the sand is smothering the water. Visitors can easily wade the creek, then climb the dunes to their heart's content. But wildlife abounds here—there are 135 species of birds and a large mammal population, too.

A new Visitors Center has exhibits that explain the formation of the dunes. Like White Sands, these dunes offer an endless excuse to use up your color film. The sand changes hue constantly, as shadows move, clouds pass, and the light varies.

Great Sand Dunes National Monument
S Colorado. Area: 57 sq. mi., 13 mi. N. of Alamosa.
Season: year round; trailer sites.

Joshua Tree National Monument ARIZONA

Though named for the Joshua Tree, a rare 40-foot member of the lily family with many-tufted branches, this big national monument in southern California preserves 870 square miles of the Mojave and Sonoran Deserts. Here grow pinyons and junipers among the rock formations of the Little San Bernardino Mountains, and strange forms of cacti in the low-lying Pinto Basin, where prehistoric Indians hunted 5,000 years ago. Numerous animals thrive in this wild, arid land. Rodents like the little pocket mouse, one of the country's tiniest, get water by eating plants that absorb it. The desert bighorn, mule deer, coyote, and mountain lion can drink at the occasional oases.

Joshua Tree National Monument lies about 150 miles from Los Angeles, halfway to the Arizona border south of route 66. Good roads cut across the desert tract and lead to points of interest. From Salton View motorists can see snow-topped San Gorgonio Mountain to the west, and look down on San Andreas Fault, birthplace of many earthquakes. Far to the south they can glimpse the Salton Sea, 235 feet below sea level.

The park service recommends that visitors carry water, for the desert is hot in summer, and a person can sweat away up to a quart of water an hour. Meals and lodging can be had at Twentynine Palms, on the northern edge. There are seven campgrounds within the monument. Bring your own wood, however, if you are interested in cooking out.

Joshua tree is a species of lily, but can top 40 feet.

Saguaro National Monument ARIZONA

Saguaro, giant of the cactus family, thrives where many plants would perish—in the blistering heat of the Sonoran Desert. Saguaros are rare enough in the United States so that a "forest" of them just 16 miles east of Tucson, Arizona, has been designated a national monument and draws thousands of motorists to gaze at the spiky, many-armed monsters that tower sometimes 50 feet.

The saguaro's habits are as strange as its looks. Its internal fibers soak up water like a sponge and store it away to nourish the plant through long droughts. When rain falls a big plant may absorb a ton of water, its outer "rib cage" distending to hold the bulging reservoir, then gradually shrinking in girth like a squeezed accordion as dry weather returns.

Thorns fend off most desert animals who would chew through the tough skin to get a drink. But ground squirrels use the spikes as a ladder to reach branch tips where saguaro fruit ripens. Birds peck out nests in the plant's flesh.

Spring is the season for a visit to the monument, for then the desert is in bloom and the 99-square-mile area sparkles with color.

Pleated saguaro swells with rain, shrinks with drought.

A sea of white dunes covers Tularosa Basin. This aerial view makes them seem small but some are 100 feet high.

White Sands National Monument NEW MEXICO

It isn't sand, really. It's gypsum, pure white, powdery, covering 275 square miles with restless dunes. You find it in the Tularosa Basin of southern New Mexico—a gleaming desert of soft, rippling gypsum.

This strange deposit is constantly refreshed from Lake Lucerno, a vast basin that dry air reduces to a gypsum-caked marsh for much of the year. Fed by runoff from surrounding mountains, Lucerno receives tons of gypsum in solution as it is washed down from exposed strata in the upper slopes. When the water evaporates, crystals remain. The wind does the rest, pulverizing the crystals and building the endless powdery dunes.

The lake and most of the dunes lie in White Sands National Monument, one of the Park Service's unique areas. You can't camp here—the town of Alamogordo is only 15 miles away. But you can drive along a self-guiding tour, picnic amid the white waves of gypsum, and best of all clamber over them and tumble down them to your heart's content, for here is a natural feature that you can't possibly hurt. Watch for lizards that have evolved ghostly white coloration after centuries of living in this white world.

White Sands National Monument
Season: year round. No accommodations.
15 mi. from Alamagordo.

Petrified Forest National Monument ARIZONA

Northern Arizona is a strange land, barren to some eyes, magically beautiful to those who really look at it. Here are stark buttes jutting from the desert, or the flat line of a mesa gullied by raw canyons. And here is a panoply of colors–reds, pinks, purples, yellows – some savagely bright, some subtle, all as elusive as the shifting light that plays on them. Only in a piece of petrified wood are these endless hues locked up so a person can gaze at them to his heart's content, even touch them.

The world's biggest, brightest collection of petrified wood lies in Arizona's Petrified Forest, on the southern rim of the Painted Desert. This is no forest of standing trees. On these 148 square miles great logs lie in jumbled scatterings. They look like dead trees waiting to be cleared by a forestry crew. But instead of wood, they are stone. Many glitter with color as though inlaid with bright jewels.

How did it all happen? The answer, say geologists, gives a remarkable glimpse of the earth as it was 170 million years ago, in the Triassic Period. These trees, a primitive species of conifer, grew then along wide, sluggish rivers that wound through what is now the arid Southwest. Dying of fire, disease, or old age, they toppled on the flat banks of the river. Periodic flooding swept them, a few at a time, downstream. And here, where ancient rivers traversed broad flood-plains, many grounded and were buried in mud.

As centuries passed, layer after layer of sediment piled on top of the dead trunks. Silica, dissolved in water, was carried into the logs where minute crystals formed and grew within the dead cells and gradually filled them. Thus, clear quartz

Broken petrified tree trunks litter the Arizona landscape in a desert area where not even sage brush can grow.

The muted pinks of northern Arizona's Painted Desert can be seen in the distance along the horizon under a typical desert sky.

preserved the wood fiber, duplicating it in every detail—splinters, knots, stubs of shattered branches and sheared-off roots. Where iron, carbon, and manganese oxide were contained in the silica-laden waters, they stained the fossil wood in brilliant colors.

Around 60 million years ago a series of vast upheavals—each an almost imperceptible lifting of the earth's crust—formed the Rocky Mountains. Thousands of years of constant erosion wore down the overlying layers of rock and entombed the stone logs. Geologists call this layer the Chinle formation. There they lie today, mummified by the ages, perfect in every feature. Some protrude from wrinkled hummocks of Chinle, some stretch across gullies to form natural bridges, some are balanced on slender pedestals of earth. Most are stripped of bark and branches, indicating that they tumbled downstream quite a distance before coming to rest. New pieces constantly crop up, but the rangers stress that the supply is limited and no one is allowed to take home a souvenir.

No two chunks are alike; no color patterns match. Visitors to Petrified Forest (and there are many on a summer day) find an endless variety of bright agatized wood to marvel at, huge trees, some 160 feet long, to walk on, new discoveries awaiting them beyond every hillock of claylike Chinle. Everyone is fooled by the so-called silicate logs whose drab hue so exactly mimics the look of old dead wood. Some trunks appear to have been sawed into neat lengths as if for pulpwood. Some seem surely to have been chopped—there are the chips, looking as though the sap were still damp. But the chips are dry and heavy and harder than steel. And even after all this, a tourist will stoop to touch a splinter because he knows that *this,* at least, is real wood. But it too is stone.

Petrified Forest is one of the easiest national park areas to visit, since it straddles both U. S. Highways 66 and 180. Branching from the highway, a park road leads to five of the six areas where the petrified wood is clustered. The sixth section, Black Forest, lies north of the highway in the Painted Desert, and can only be reached on foot—a long hike. The Rainbow Forest Visitor Center Museum presents the story of the formation of petrified wood and displays brilliant, polished cross sections.

Ancient Indians used the chunks to build a pueblo here. The ruins remain. And they scratched an array of drawings on a big, flat-faced boulder aptly named Newspaper Rock. It's well worth pausing to "read" this imperishable tabloid.

Petrified Forest National Monument
E-central Arizona. Area: 147 sq. mi.
Accessible by US 66 or 260.

Mesa Verde National Park COLORADO

In the southwestern corner of Colorado a 15- by 20-mile tabletop mountain rises 1,000 to 2,000 feet above the surrounding land. Since it is well covered by those plateau evergreens, juniper and piñon, the Spanish named it Mesa Verde: Green Table. Father Escalante camped on the Manlos River, a few miles to the east, while he was exploring toward the Colorado River in 1776. But few explorers bothered to climb to the mesa's slanting top. After all, it seemed the same as hundreds of other mesas in this rugged, eroded land.

Mesa Verde *is* much the same. But it is riddled with canyons where wind, and millenniums of rain scoured channels running off the mesa from north to south. The upper canyon walls are niched by caves – broad undercuts where rock flaked away over the centuries. The caves, in turn, contain hundreds of little stone houses.

There are more of these masonry dwellings on the fingers of high land between canyons. There are more, in fact, than anyone has ever counted. More are surveyed all the time.

Who built them? Prehistoric Indians who farmed the Mesa Verde for over a thousand years and developed a fascinating culture. Their structures–single dwellings, and villages of attached homes with watchtowers, storerooms, and underground ceremonial chambers–are found throughout Arizona and New Mexico, and in southern Utah and Colorado, and northern Mexico as well. The Spanish called their neat and compact settlements pueblos, and we speak of these native Americans as Pueblo Indians.

Their buildings were discovered one by one by Anglo-American settlers in the late 19th century. The most spectacular finds–whole towns that had lain forgotten and undisturbed for 700 years, did, naturally, show the effects of centuries of neglect. The ancient architects had no knowledge of bonding walls or of placing their structures upon foundations. And while some opportunists among the 19th century prospectors dug among the dwellings for the prehistoric pottery that museums paid well for, with little regard for preserving the antiquities around them, most explorers were genuinely interested in the ruins. Thanks to these men, American archaeology developed as a science and we learned to respect and preserve our antiquities.

Luckily, Mesa Verde became a national park in time to stop its total devastation. What remains – the cliff dwellings and mesa-top buildings –

Cliff Palace, the largest Mesa Verde ruin, was once a town of 400 people before it was abandoned in the 13th century. Circular walls in the foreground held kivas, ceremonial meeting places for men; the square rooms were dwellings and storehouses.

have a serene dignity that makes hundreds of thousands of annual visitors wonder, fleetingly, if Pueblo life wasn't in some ways more attractive than the turmoil of modern civilization.

You enter Mesa Verde National Park from the north on a spectacular road that clings to the mesa wall, winding toward the top. It leads to the park headquarters area at Spruce Canyon. Here you will find cabins, campground, a restaurant, and Spruce Tree Lodge. Check with the Mesa Verde Co., Mesa Verde National Park, Colorado, for reservations if you plan to stay under a roof.

Mesa Verde's caves are undercuts caused by water seepage. Freezing and thawing flakes away the soft sandstone. This is Long House ruin before recent excavation by archeologists.

The first place to visit is the park museum where Indian prehistory is explained with the aid of five dioramas that cover 15,000 years. From here, when the sites are open, ranger-guided trail trips lead to Spruce Tree House, the best preserved of Mesa Verde's sites.

This is a village containing 114 dwelling rooms and eight kivas (ceremonial chambers) set under the overhang of a canyon-wall cave. Some of the high walls go clear to the roof of the cave. Many of the ceilings, made of timbered beams, cut poles, and adobe, are intact.

Looping drives lead you to additional sites. You can drive close to Cliff Palace, the biggest and best-known of all the ruins, with its complex of rooms—accommodation for 400 people—and its four-story tower. Skimming the edge of another canyon, your road passes Balcony House, famed for its defensive design. Here, accompanied by a ranger, you can climb a ladder up the canyon wall to a ledge that leads along the rear of the cave to the court in the midst of the ancient dwellings. You will notice the wall that was built with careful stonework to safeguard the outer edge of the court. It is not the work of the park service, but of Pueblo Indians, a thousand years ago, who didn't like the idea of their adventurous youngsters tumbling into the canyon.

The only way out of Balcony House is through the crawl tunnel, a narrow opening barely big enough for one tourist to crawl through at a time. This was the only means of entrance for the original owners—a clever foil against invaders.

There are hundreds more cliff dwellings. Mesa Verde's Indians took to the caves late in their period of habitation, when raids by nomadic Indians threatened their communities. Earlier they lived in open sites atop the mesa and close to their farm lands and hunting grounds. Archaeologists have suggested that bad farming methods, enemy pressure, inter-village disputes, and a long drought toward the end of the 13th century probably were factors in the break-up of their culture. The agricultural Pueblos may have been easy prey for the roaming bands of hunters and looters that had come from the northeast to explore this territory. These invaders are thought to have been members of the Shoshonean tribes who wandered southward from Canada east of the Rockies, then veered into the Southwest.

Mystery surrounds the Sun Temple, a ruin on top of the mesa that dates from the late years of Pueblo civilization. You wind by the ruin on a second loop road that goes south from the headquarters area.

Park-approved trails lead visitors around and through the maze of wild canyons that slice Mesa Verde. If you hike you must get a permit. The going is tough, and the rangers need to know where you're headed. But on these trails you will find the joy of solitude, for the great majority of tourists stick to the roads.

To help relieve the pressure of visitors at Mesa Verde's old and famous sites, the Wetherill Mesa area, west of park headquarters, is being excavated and developed. It is not open to visitors and will probably not be accessible for several years. It will be worth waiting for, however, for it is rich in archeology, and contains the second largest dwelling in the park, Long House.

Though the park is open all year, activities such as guided trips and campfire talks are carried on from early June to mid-September only. Accommodations, including the campground, and horse rentals are for summer. But you may drive through the park as long as the roads are not blocked by snow and ice. And if you do, take a camera. Few sights are more beautiful than the view of a cliff dwelling shrouded in snow.

Mesa Verde National Park
SW Colorado. Area: 51,300 acres.
Season: May-Oct. for guided trips. Open year round.
Accommodations: camping sites, trailer park, cabins.
Services: museum, trail trips, horse rental in summer.
US highway 160 leads to park road.

The Ancient Indians of the Southwest

by ALEX SPEARS

The dry canyon country of northern Arizona and New Mexico contains hundreds of Indian ruins—cliff dwellings, open-site pueblos, individual dwellings—dating from the great era of Pueblo civilization. A few of the finest of these ancient villages have become incorporated in national monuments and national parks. A great many others lie along remote canyons, seldom visited, forgotten by present-day Pueblo Indians, slowly crumbling with the passing centuries.

The following story deals with a typical pueblo of the early 13th century. Though it is ficticious, and does not apply to any particular village, it attempts to follow the known facts about those peaceable and kindly people.

The morning sun had grown hot, beating into the canyon with almost physical pressure. The boy stabbed listlessly with his digging stick at the caked soil of the village garden. His mind was far from the corn and squash growing there, and he really didn't care if the weeds grew or not. He rested and gazed longingly at the line of cottonwoods and walnuts that marked the line of the creek, 100 paces away. Sweat dampened his red-brown skin, but evaporated so quickly in the dry air that he felt no cooling effect from it—only a great thirst.

He was a stocky 15-year-old, bare except for a cotton cloth tied to his waist. His black hair hung to his shoulders. He was tired. He seemed to be tired most of the time, according to his mother.

The thought of her made him glance up quickly at the village. It stretched along its deep, shadowy cave in the canyon wall, 40 feet above his head, and he saw with relief that his own doorway, far to the left on the second level, did not frame her figure. For once she was not making note of his laziness and planning a punishment for him that evening. She might have gone next door for a visit, or perhaps she was inside, replastering the cracked adobe behind the cooking fire.

That was good. He could rest a minute. His father had scaled the cliff early in the morning to go hunting on the mesa-tops with some cronies. He wouldn't be home until dusk. Anyway, his father just told him how many garden rows to cultivate and left it up to his mother to see that he did it.

So he stood still, breathing the hot, clear air and staring up at the village, so cool and inviting. Wisps of blue smoke wreathed over its neatly aligned homes and storerooms, and deepened the cool shadow that fell on it all through the summer's heat. Familiar sounds echoed down from the arched roof of the cave. There was the scrape of a twig broom as some housewife swept her patio, the snap of twigs being broken for a cooking fire. He could hear women's voices gossiping from door to door, a quick burst of laughter. And behind all these was the steady scrape of corn being ground to meal in the metates and the sweet humming of the grinding songs.

Then the peace was shattered by a stream of small children, shouting and chasing each other up a ladder to the second level, then along an uneven line of roofs, in and out of a tall storehouse, down another ladder to the plaza on the cave floor, and past a group of kivas. Only here did the screaming

and giggling fade for a moment, for everyone knew that down in those underground chambers dwelt a mystery, that there the elders decided profound village business, that even now they might be planning a ceremony.

Safely past the ladders jutting up from the kivas' entrances, the game continued, naked youngsters racing up to the rear of the cave. One infant still in juniper bark diapers tottered toward his house ladder, determined to follow, but his mother snatched him back, laughing at him. At the turkey pen, built against the rear wall, the children stopped, their game forgotten at the prospect of teasing the birds. Squawks and gobbles now rebounded from the cave. Dogs appeared from nowhere, tails wagging, wolflike ears cocked. And then the useless old man who turned the turkeys loose each morning shuffled into sight, shouting and waving his stick, and the dogs and children fled.

The boy grinned as he watched. It hadn't been too long since he had run naked and yelled at the top of his lungs, and fought gloriously, especially with girls, and driven all the grown-ups to distraction. Life had been nice, then. He had eaten what he wanted and slept when he was tired, simply curling up in some corner of the cave. Everyone took care of him—his mother, of course, and all his mother's clan, and all her women friends, too. He was allowed to do just about anything he wanted.

He sighed, partly from the heat, and partly from sorrow at his lost childhood, and returned grimly to his task. And then he saw the girl.

She was walking past the garden on her way to the creek, a black and white water jar under one arm. And though he had known her all his life—had raced her and fought her and played with her and screamed at her—he felt now that he had never seen her before. She was wearing her hair like a grown woman! He remembered that she had recently been through the puberty rites—such festivals were the talk of the village—but he hadn't realized what a touch of growing up, in dress and hairstyle, would do to her—or to him.

There was something about her walk, a slight hesitation, a sway. And she gripped the jar as she had the feathered stick that he had once teased her about, but now her brown arms seemed softer,

rounder. She glanced over at him, but instead of mocking him with an insult as she would have last week, she just smiled faintly. Her lips seemed redder. And her eyes certainly were bigger.

Suddenly the boy threw down his digging stick in disgust. This job was too dull to be bothered with. He was far too big and strong to be wasting his life like this. He looked defiantly up at the village again to see if his mother was watching—not that he was afraid of her, but just to see. She wasn't.

Holding himself in such a way that his chest muscles looked very big, and turning his arms so his biceps showed up, he stepped over the planted rows toward the creek. She was still filling the jar when he reached it. She seemed to be having trouble getting the right amount of water into it, first too much, and then when she slopped some out there wouldn't be enough. She paid no attention to him, and he strenuously avoided her, flopping down for a drink some yards away.

The water was delightful on his hot face. He sloshed some over his torso. It felt good, and it made his muscles gleam in what he fancied a most picturesque way.

After a moment, the girl got the jar filled just right and turned back toward the village. The boy saw what he had to do, even if it was woman's work. He jumped up, overtook her, and plucked the jar from her hands. She looked full at him, and her eyes were definitely bigger.

"I'll carry it," he mumbled quickly.

"Oh, no, you don't have to."

"I don't mind. Come on."

She hesitated. "It's so nice and cool in the shade. Let's wait for a moment."

He set the jar down and stood for just an instant beside her. Then she darted away to pick a small white flower with four petals. She brought it back to show him.

"These are lucky," she told him. "I think the earth-god leaves them just for me."

He laughed. "You shouldn't be talking about gods. You're just a woman."

"And you shouldn't be carrying water, you're just a boy."

"A man," he said. "And if you don't want me to . . ."

"I don't mind," she answered. "I'll carry my flower. Come on."

First wait a moment, then hurry up, the boy thought. Women are strange. He picked up the jar and they walked rather stiffly together to the cave ladder. He scrambled up, holding the jar as best he could, and he was painfully aware that this time his mother *was* watching, stick in hand.

"You'll be punished for leaving the garden," the girl said, mounting the ladder behind him.

"I don't care," he said, and almost meant it.

The coolness of the cave wrapped around him as he reached the floor and waited for the girl. The cooking fires smelled of juniper and piñon, of rabbit stew and corn cakes. The sounds and voices echoed pleasantly under the ruddy sandstone arch. One of the voices was his mother's, calling his name. He pretended not to hear, but the neighbors heard and began poking their heads from their T-shaped doorways, watching and grinning.

The girl led the way to her dwelling. He came behind, embarrassed. And just as he reached her door the jar slipped from his sweaty hands and shattered on the cave floor with a great splash of precious water.

All he could do was stare at it numbly. The girl was screaming at him as though it had been a week ago and never any puberty rites. The girl's mother was screaming at the girl. And if that wasn't bad enough, the rest of the village was howling with laughter.

Head down, the boy turned toward his own home. Long training had taught him that if he was due for a punishment, he'd get it, and it might as well be over and done with. But when he reached his house, he stopped dumbfounded. Instead of scowling at him, his mother was smiling.

"You are a man," she said. "You are like your father. And you will be leaving my house sooner than I had thought."

She held out her arms to him, as though on an impulse. And on an impulse he went to her and hugged her as he had not done for a long time. For a moment he wanted to cry—but he was a man.

"Go help the girl and her mother clean up the mess," his mother said. "Then come back and eat some stew. The garden can wait."

He blushed a little again when he presented himself at the girl's house. But she had gone for more water, and her mother just smiled at him and handed over a broom. He swept the fragments of the water jar over the edge of the cliff, and they tumbled onto the talus slope of stone rubble and broken pottery that lay below the village.

That evening, as the boy returned home, he found his fatigue forgotten in the strange excitement that had stirred within him since his mother had spoken of manhood. She had talked of his leaving her house. Surely she didn't think he was man enough yet to marry the girl and move in to her home, as a husband must? No, there was another possibility, but it was so exciting a prospect that he hardly dared consider it.

The canyon was almost in shadow, and the cave glowed with the lights of many fires as he walked its paths to his dwelling. He passed babies in their cradle boards, fretting for supper as they hung on roof poles, swinging gently back and forth. He passed a row of fresh jars, just fashioned by some woman, and set out to dry before being fired—and the sight made him feel uncomfortable. A group of hunters, back from a long trip on the mesa-top, were playing a gambling game for choice cuts of meat. He wondered how the gods had treated his own father—whether there would be another rabbit stew for supper or a chunk of venison.

It was venison. His father had beaten him home, dragging along a fine young doe. Already his mother had it trussed over the outdoor fire, and the neighbors were arriving to share the feast. The food smells aroused his hunger and he watched impatiently while the meat was cooked and sliced and served, along with corn meal cakes. As he sank his teeth into it he felt he had never tasted food before.

The meal passed quickly and silently except for the slurps and finger-suckings and rumbling belches that signified praise for the cook and well-mannered thanks for the repast. And later, when the young children were asleep, his father came over to where he sat, perched at the edge of the cave, staring down into the moonlit canyon.

"Your mother has told me what a fine water carrier you are," his father said, smiling.

The boy stirred uneasily, and grinned a little.

"You might try your hand at hunting, now," his father continued. "Six of us are going toward the sacred mountain tomorrow. You may come if you want." Then seriously. "But you must promise to stay with me at all times. Today I thought I saw signal smoke. The enemy may be planning another raid. You are young and have sharp eyes. Tell me if you see anything strange. Meanwhile, until we are sure, do not alarm the others."

The boy looked up in eagerness. Then he frowned at a sudden thought. "What about the crops, Father?"

The man laughed aloud. "By the gods you thought of the garden. Your mother is right. Manhood is coming to you. Don't worry, my son. There are many other youths such as you have been until today who can do the tasks of the village garden. You will learn to guard the village. And soon now you will leave home to sleep in the kiva."

So that was what his mother had meant, after all! The kiva—refuge of the men, house of religion and sometimes revelry, dormitory for bachelors. He could hear a ceremony going on in one of them now—the muffled drumming of feet on the sounding boards to tell the spirits that men wished to communicate with them. Sponsored by his uncle, he had taken part in rituals and knew the secrets of the gods and seen the sipapu—the earth hole in the kiva floor through which the spirits emerge. Now he would move in with other young men and sleep among the gods.

He nodded happily at his father and gazed about him at the village that suddenly he loved so well.

* * *

A thousand years later, national park rangers still try to explain the mysteries of the kiva and its sipapu and foot drums. They show visitors the silent cave dwellings. They point out the creek and where the garden lay. And they display fragments of black and white pottery, gathered from the rubbish heaps that slant away from the cliff below the village.

Visitors walk away with a feeling that life here must still continue, somehow, behind their backs. And, stooping, a woman may see a small white flower with four petals. It's Utah's state flower, the sego lily.

Pueblo Bonito, with 800 dwellings, is the largest Indian ruin in the United States. It was deserted 700 years ago.

Chaco Canyon National Monument NEW MEXICO

Northwestern New Mexico is dry range land, rolling gently, sometimes rising gradually to break off in burnished cliffs, sometimes cut by broad, flat-floored valleys. Chaco Canyon is one of these, a wide ribbon sunk between shallow walls in a sunny, secluded pocket of land. A man could do worse than live in such a place.

Centuries ago, Indians thought the same thing. While Europeans were groping through their Dark Ages, a group of farmers settled in this bright and happy valley, dug primitive pit houses, tilled the canyon floor, and gradually built up a thriving culture. It reached its high point with the magnificent walled town, Pueblo Bonito, that forms the focal point of Chaco Canyon National Monument.

A true wonder of the world, this "beautiful village" stands four stories tall in some places, has two broad plazas, 32 kivas, 800 dwellings, and many storage rooms. It forms the shape of a "D," spreading over three acres—the biggest open-site Indian ruin in the national park system. Until the 1880's it ranked as the largest apartment house the world had ever seen.

When the West's first scenic photographer, William H. Jackson, explored Chaco Canyon in 1877, he found his best view of Pueblo Bonito on the lip of the north wall of the canyon. A shaky old Indian stairway led up to this overlook: below spread the ruin, mostly buried in sand.

The same stairway, considerably strengthened by the park service, leads to the same vantage point today. But the view is much better. Seven expeditions by the National Geographic Society cleared 100,000 tons of dirt off the site and exposed its true size and complexity. The curve of the "D" tucks close under the cliff and stands 40 feet high, embracing the clustering dwellings and storerooms. The plazas stretch away to the low wall along the "D"'s straight line. They are pocked by the circular kivas where menfolk of the village would meet for ceremonies—and to socialize together for an evening, away from their wives and children.

The cliff view gives you a fine overall glimpse of the great structure, but you must walk through it to appreciate the love and care that went into it. Sections of the walls were built with skill and sophistication: a straight line of neatly cut sandstone, then several layers of small slabs, then another course of wide blocks, and so on, all meticulously fitted to stand without mortar. Ventilation ducts cut through the dwelling chambers to draw off the smoke of indoor fires. Some rooms retain their original ceilings of evenly spaced round beams holding a cross layer of tight-packed poles. These hold the adobe roof. Ceilings are low and doors small—these early Pueblo Indians were short in stature.

Rangers point out many interior doorways that have been sealed up with masonry. The Indians, not the park service, did this for reasons of their own. Windows and doors in the outer wall are frequently blocked up the same way, for Pueblo Bonito had to defend itself from those roving bands of hunters and raiders, the forefathers of today's Navajos and Apaches.

Pueblo Bonito is only one of several Indian ruins along an eight-mile stretch of Chaco Canyon. There are others like Una Vida and Chettro Kettle, each a small town in its day. And across the valley is Casa Rinconada, dating from about 1100 A.D., where self-guiding tour signs point out the evolution of the first primitive settlers into pueblo builders. Around 900 A.D., work began on Pueblo Bonito. Its culture reached its zenith at about the time William the Conqueror sailed for England. Drought and the overworked soil drove the citizens away at about the end of the 13th century.

The small rock hawk thrives in dry areas. It subsists on a diet of rodents and insects.

Bandelier National Monument NEW MEXICO

Years of drought and, perhaps, raids by nomadic Indians ended the golden age of Pueblo civilization in the 13th century. Cultural centers like Mesa Verde and Chaco Canyon gradually became ghost towns. Their citizens moved to safer spots where the grass was still green. One such location was Frijoles Canyon in the Rio Grande Valley, near Santa Fe, New Mexico. There, the Pueblo refugees built a handsome walled town, Tyuonyi. Its ruins are the focal point of today's Bandelier National Monument, named for the Swiss-American archeologist who wrote *The Delight Makers.*

Frijoles Canyon cuts deep into a broad plateau mostly made up of compressed volcanic ash, called tuff. Winding through the canyon is a little brook with a lilting name, El Rito de los Frijoles—in English it's just plain Bean Creek—which supplied water for the 14th-century community that developed here.

Tyuonyi was built beside the creek. It was a roughly circular communal dwelling, its outside wall windowless for protection from raiders. Its living rooms and store rooms rose two or three stories against the inside of the wall. To enter his home, an Indian climbed up on the roof and let himself down a ladder into his own chamber.

In the center of the village stretched an open courtyard with kivas, or ceremonial rooms, sunk into it. The plan is not unlike Pueblo Bonito at Chaco Canyon National Monument. Although no direct connection has been established, there appears to have been some influence in the Rio Grande from the Chaco area.

Tyuonyi contained about 400 rooms. Other homes were built against the base of the canyon wall, and many neat cave rooms were gouged out of the soft turf of the cliff itself. These, however, were of secondary importance in most structures, for they appear to be the back rooms of the small masonry buildings erected in front of the cliff face.

The cliff rooms of Bandelier remain in almost perfect condition, their walls blackened by the smoke of ancient cooking fires, their floors smoothed by thousands of sweepings by Pueblo housewives. Park visitors can climb up to the rooms and sit in their doorways, and enjoy this high view of Tyuonyi's ruin, spreading below on the canyon floor.

The Frijoles Canyon settlement was probably still active when Coronado passed through the area in 1540, but the Spaniard left no record of having seen it. About 40 years later Tyuonyi and its cliffside suburbs were deserted. It is possible that the small water supply could not supply the population.

Visitors today may either camp or stay at a lodge that is near the Park Service visitor center and museum.

Chaco Canyon National Monument
NW New Mexico. Area: 32 sq. mi.
Season: year round. Trailer space.
Climate: frequent rain, hot days, cool nights.

Bandelier National Monument
N-central New Mexico. Area: 31,000 acres.
Season: year round. Campgrounds,lodge.

Tuonyi, like Pueblo Bonito, was an open-site walled town. As it grew, new residents added more rings of rooms.

An Indian guide stops at the only fresh water spring along the path to Keet Seel.

Navajo National Monument ARIZONA

One of the nation's last truly wild areas is the Navajo Reservation of northern Arizona. Few roads cut through this high, empty plateau country, but many remote and little-known canyons do, rich with surprises for those able to explore them. Navajo National Monument consists of three beautifully preserved and spectacular pre-Columbian Indian ruins—complete villages, hidden away from the white man's civilization.

You need a little nerve and muscle to see these three sites, Keet Seel, Betatakin, and Inscription House. No superhighway leads to monument headquarters, but the rough and sometimes exciting road that winds uphill from the trading post of Shonto gives you (and presumably your car) a sense of accomplishment. No luxurious tourist lodge awaits you at the end of the trip, only a campground among fragrant junipers and piñons.

There's no air conditioning, but you'll breathe the crisp air of more than a mile of altitude. There's no television, but the stars here are very big, and the far-reaching, night-long stillness of the plateau is a fine thing to listen to. Breakfast doesn't come on a waiter's tray, but in your own frying pan. Horses are easy to acquire and almost a necessity if you want to visit Keet Seel. You *must* go either on horseback or on foot, and it's a long walk—about 8 miles each way.

The trail leads right over the lip of Segi Canyon and down its 1,000-foot wall in a series of steep switchbacks. Your Navajo pony knows how to take this trail—you don't. So sit back, grip your saddle horn, and if necessary shut your eyes as your horse hops from ledge to ledge, pivots with his neck stretched out over the abyss, slips, scrambles, side-steps, blows, and groans. He'll get you down to the canyon floor—and once there you will be rewarded by a clear, rippling stream, patches of brilliant green grass, thickets of aspens with whispering leaves, and the silent peace of this natural highway so far from the thunder of modern traffic.

The path winds along the floor of a branch canyon, passes a little waterfall where you can take a drink from the only good spring within miles, then enters a wider section carpeted with rank grass. Beyond, in the northern wall of the canyon is a deep niche 100 yards long, its streaked ceiling curving up to blend with the cliff face. An uneven jumble of rectangles lines the bottom of this natural alcove and as you approach, these shapes begin to make sense: You are looking at a complete village—dwellings, silos, kivas, watch towers, their bleak, lifeless windows dark against the pale masonry walls. This is Keet Seel ("Broken Pottery"), the largest cave dwelling in Arizona, a town of 160 rooms that lay forgotten for 600 years and still seems ready to begin life again where it left off.

A 40-foot ladder takes you to the village "street" of Keet Seel, and you can walk the length of the town, peer into the dwellings, and recapture the flavor of its life. Inside the T-shaped doorways are small, square rooms plastered with adobe, sooty from the smoke of thousands of ancient cooking fires. Near the door you may see a metate holding a worn grinding stone. In a storeroom you may find dried corn cobs. Along the back of the cavern are splotches of ancient guano. These mark the pens where Keet Seel's original residents kept wild turkeys. Everywhere you will feel a sense of expectancy: these rooms must surely be waiting for their residents to return. You will find that your voice is lower than normal,

Betatakin clings to the steep floor of a colossal, stagelike cave. Here visitors examine some homes and small storerooms standing near the cave's edge. Many buildings have collapsed. Betatakin's town spring still flows out front.

Keet Seel is largest of Arizona's cliff ruins. Run-off water streaks the cliff face with mineral oxides.

as though you were trespassing. When you climb down the ladder, remount your pony, and jog away, you'll have the feeling that as soon as you are out of sight Keet Seel again stirs and glimmers with fresh fires and rings with the sound of voices, the hum of prayer, the squeals of happy, naked, brown-skinned babies playing in the sun.

Betatakin, the second great cliff dwelling at Navajo National Monument, is easier to reach from headquarters. A short hike leads to an overlook from where you can gaze across a deep canyon to a huge, vaulting cave, cut from the cliff wall by water freezing and flaking away the rock over the centuries. The symmetrical arch is big enough to cover the Capitol at Washington (like Rainbow Bridge). On its slanting floor early Pueblo Indians built their village—about 100 rooms, perfectly sheltered from weather, shaded in summer's heat, but open to the winter sun.

From the overlook, the town looks small and rather drab against its spectacular stage setting. But when you wind down the canyon trail to the cave and climb up among those fine stone buildings, you are in a town nearly as impressive as Keet Seel.

The third ruin of this trio is Inscription House, 33 miles from headquarters by road. Again, you will have to walk down into its canyon to find this small, high-perched cliff dwelling. It gets its name from the date, 1661, found scratched on a wall when the pueblo was found in 1909. The early date must have come from some wandering Spanish explorer.

Navajo National Monument

NE Arizona. Area: 520 acres.
Season: year round.
Climate: hot days, cool nights.
Accommodations: camp sites, trailer space.
Services: horse rental.
Park is south of Kayenta on State highway 64.

Canyon de Chelly National Monument ARIZONA

Three broad, irregular canyons, coming together to form one, fashion a leaf-shaped scar on the map of northeastern Arizona. They are Canyon de Chelly (pronounced Shay), Canyon del Muerto, and Monument Canyon. All three cut deeply into the plateau with vertical walls of gleaming red sandstone. Their wide, level floors are dry sand washes most of the year, but sometimes rains turn them into muddy torrents. Cottonwood groves lend shade to their peaceful, secluded pockets.

Together, the three canyons make up Canyon de Chelly National Monument. Breathtaking beauty and the preservation of ruins are not the only reasons that this site is preserved by the Park Service. For here is an ancient and traditional home of the Navajo Indians. Here they live much as they have for centuries, almost undisturbed by white man's civilization beyond the canyon walls.

Mummy Cave housed Indians for over 1,000 years.

Visitors to Canyon de Chelly may camp at the monument headquarters or stay at privately owned Thunderbird Ranch, near monument headquarters. Horses or a specially equipped sightseeing car make trips through the vast, rock-walled avenues. These tours bring visitors face to face with the secretive, half-forgotten canyon world. No one should make a trip into Canyon de Chelly on his own, for there are a few spots of quicksand.

Tours avoid these pitfalls and bring you close to the round or octagonal hogans of Navajo families, each with its brush corral and a garden stretching in the shade of towering cliffs. You may see a flock of goatlike Indian sheep herded by a small, barefooted Navajo girl in a long purple velvet dress—a style adopted from the cast-off clothes of charitable army wives, late in the 19th century.

You may even be lucky enough to see a gnarled old grandmother kneeling beneath a sun shelter of cottonwood boughs, and weaving a Navajo rug. The art is dying now, as only a few young people continue it. Don't try to take her picture until your guide arranges it. Many of these elders believe that being photographed robs them of a part of themselves. If you offer fifty cents for her to pose, don't expect thanks. She will take it—but contemptuously, for she wants it clearly understood that white man's money cannot buy her friendship, nor destroy her pride. She is one of "The People," as Navajos call themselves.

Haughty and domineering these Indians may seem, but this intense racial pride has kept them not only alive but flourishing in a world that is hostile to their way of life. And if you produce the Navajo greeting, "Ya-a-tay," to the head of the hogan as he rides home on his tough little pony, you may inspire him to honor you by solemnly raising his hand. He wears faded Levis, ties his long hair with a cloth band at his neck,

White House ruin perches in a niche beneath a huge cliff. It gets its name from white clay-plastered twin towers.

and guides his cayuse by a rope rein. If he doesn't see you, he may sing while he rides—a strange, high-pitched chant that wavers up and down, sounding wild and mysterious.

If you have little children in your party, the Indian will unbend with a broad smile. Navajos love their own children, and spoil them. And though they haven't much use for white people, they can't help but grin at a white child.

The white man's world interfered with The People in the days when Spaniards roamed the Southwest. Naturally, the Navajos raided them and stole their horses whenever they could. The People are a normally nomadic group, and always used to live by hunting and preying on richer, more sedentary Indians. The Spaniards seemed like fair game.

But after one raid in 1804, Spanish troops followed the Navajos into this canyon stronghold, bottled up a group of women and children in a high cave, and killed them by firing against the roof so their bullets ricocheted into them. Lead splotches can still be seen on the ceiling of that cave in Canyon del Muerto (Canyon of Death).

Then in 1864, the famous frontiersman Kit Carson was assigned the job of rounding up troublesome Navajos and removing them to a reserve in New Mexico. Carson and his cavalrymen caught about 8,000 Indians in Canyon de Chelly and herded them off on a long, grim trek to the Bosque Redondo. But so many died in that hot and hostile concentration camp, far from the land they loved, that the government relented and let them return. And here the Navajo have lived ever since—about 300 of them now—in this sacred and secluded canyon within their own huge reservation.

The three canyons sheltered the Anasazi, the Ancient Ones, centuries before the first Navajo poked his head into them. These slickrock walls have many of the flat-floored, round-roofed caves that any visitor to the Southwest soon learns may harbor ancient Indian ruins. Sure enough there are more than 400 of them within this 131-square-mile national monument.

Mummy Cave, in Canyon del Muerto, boasts a

Susie, Sam, and Mary Reed are Navajos of Canyon de Chelly. Fine cast-silver jewelry adorns Mary's neck and ears.

fine, well-preserved dwelling with a three-story watch tower of smooth, evenly cut masonry. It stands above the remnants of pit houses that were built by Basketmaker Indians centuries before. Archeologists think this cave was inhabited from about the time that Christ was born to the drought period in about 1300. This village may have been continuously inhabited longer than any other in the United States.

Near it are Antelope House and Standing Cow, both ancient cliff dwellings, but named for Navajo paintings that still adorn the canyon walls more than a century after they were done.

The highlight of the pre-Columbian sites is White House Ruin, in Canyon de Chelly. This cliff dwelling perches high in the canyon wall and remains beautifully preserved—three stories with 80 rooms and four kivas. It gets its name from the white plaster, made from adobe, that covers a room in its top level. Since this floor is set back from the front wall, like a penthouse, it was more protected from weather by being deeper inside the cave.

So the white tower of White House Ruin glints weirdly from deep shadow. And if you go to the overlook at the lip of the canyon, you can look down almost 1,000 feet and across at the dark cave in the opposite wall, and there is White House, very tiny, its tower staring back up at you like a phosphorescent eye.

Canyon de Chelley National Monument

NE Arizona. Area: 131 sq. mi.
Season: year round.
Climate: hot days, cool nights.
Accommodations: camp site, priv. ranch accom.
Services: conducted tours, horse rental.
State highway 264 leads to park road.

Sunset Crater National Monument ARIZONA

The San Francisco Mountains, near Flagstaff, Arizona, are the highest peaks in the state. Now extinct, these volcanoes rise well over the 12,000-foot mark, pale blue giants streaked with snow even at summer's height. Motorists rushing west on Route 66 can make them out 60 miles away.

Long before white men and highways arrived that distant view guided Indians flocking here from every corner of the Southwest. The big attraction, back in the 11th century, was soil made suddenly fertile because of another volcanic eruption close by the dormant San Franciscos—an eruption that sprayed cinders and ash over 800 square miles of desert and left as its monument a small, symmetrical cinder cone—Sunset Crater.

At the time when William the Conqueror was preparing to invade England, the few, remote Indian farmers beside the San Franciscos felt the earth stirring and rumbling beneath their feet. They gathered their belongings and fled. Sure enough, the land simply blew apart. Lava gushed from deep fissures and curled through the forest, wiping out every growing thing. Cinders belched from the ground and built a 1,000-foot cone, its crater edged with bright-colored mineral deposits so that the whole summit took on the hue of a southwestern sunset.

The devastation spread for miles. But throughout the "fall-out" area, where cinders and ash blanketed the ground, the sparse rainfall was trapped and guarded from evaporation. Wild grasses shot up and the Indians realized that nature's savagery had brought its own bounty. Farmers hurried to this blackened land near the San Franciscos.

Sunset Crater, the cause of it all, has not rumbled for 900 years, nor has it changed much from the days when it was formed. The national monument road leading to the ruddy-tipped black pyramid changes from an asphalt dirt to a cinder surface. The forest floor turns black. Quickly you enter another world—one of darkness and apparent vast devastation.

Don't try to pitch a tent. Pegs won't hold in

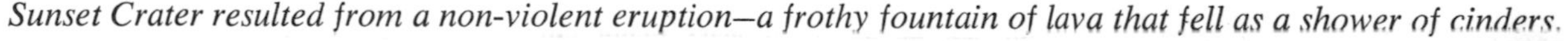

Sunset Crater resulted from a non-violent eruption—a frothy fountain of lava that fell as a shower of cinders.

The horned toad is actually a shy and harmless lizard. He escapes the desert's noon heat by burying himself in the sand.

the cinders. But do take time to explore the Bonito Lava Flow if you have old boots with sturdy soles. Those jumbled chunks underfoot are glass-sharp.

Small spatter cones dot the hard black flow, each a miniature volcano. Sharp, curling ridges of lava are squeeze-ups—they were pushed up through open cracks in the lava flow.

Most visitors climb the crater, though the ankle-deep cinders make for hard going. But the view from the top is magnificent: the lava winding away from the base of the cone—most volcanoes spill lava from their sides, not their craters—the stark and beautiful landscape, and above all the great San Francisco peaks looking down on their violent little offspring.

Walnut Canyon National Monument ARIZONA

This wooded little canyon, about 10 miles from Flagstaff, was already a settled community when Sunset Crater's eruption brought land-hungry Indians to the area. Walnut Canyon's geological structure made it a natural site for cliff dwellings. Limestone ledges form long, straight shelves along the walls, so all that the Indians had to do, a thousand years ago, was wall up the front of these shelves, partition their dwellings, and move in. The land rush boosted population to more than 300 attached houses, as neat as a Baltimore residential street.

Walnut Canyon's deep gorge abounds with Indian ruins perched on its limestone ledges.

Walnut Canyon is only about 400 feet deep, but its walls are so steep that its dwellings are hard to reach, except for those on the "Island." This is a butte rising from the canyon floor, shelved with the same limestone ledges, and completely ringed by houses. Visitors stepping out the back door of the national monument visitor center look down on the Island with its row of rectangular doorways. An easy trail leads to it along a spur that reaches out like a causeway.

Until Walnut Canyon became a national monument in 1915, this easy access to the Island almost ruined the ruins. "Pot-hunters," looking for artifacts that sometimes fetched good prices from archeologists, raided the rooms and kicked over many masonry walls.

The Park Service has restored what it can. Its museum exhibits give a clear picture of life here in prehistoric times.

Wupatki National Monument ARIZONA

Prevailing southwest winds spread most of Sunset Crater's ash and cinders over the desert land northeast of the volcano, stretching to the Little Colorado River. Wupatki National Monument covers 56 square miles of this "fall-out" area, and shows the full significance of the eruption. For this normally dry region sprang to life under its black blanket and thousands of early farmers staked claims in it. Here stand more than 800 ruins, starkly impressive masonry buildings built to fit the rugged contour of the land and now weathered so that they seem almost a part of it.

Wupatki ("Tall House") is the most impressive single ruin within the monument. It's an open-site village, a small version of Pueblo Bonito. It started as a modest structure, then expanded along with the Indian population. Near it stands an amphitheater and a ball court. This court was built by migrants from southern Arizona, for the Indian ball game of those pre-Columbian days (apparently a sort of basketball) was hugely popular in the South. It came originally from the Mayas of Mexico and Central America.

Wupatki, like Sunset Crater and Walnut Canyon, is open all year, but offers no lodgings or lunch counters for visitors since it is close to both Flagstaff and Cameron. A park road connects Wupatki with Sunset Crater and leads past one of the great fortress ruins, the Citadel, that dot the national monument. Wupatki ruin is right beside monument headquarters.

Sunset Crater, Walnut Canyon, Wupatki Natl. Mon.
N central Arizona
Season: year round.
Climate: hot.
No accommodations, but near cities of Flagstaff and Cameron, Arizona.

Wupatki, a short drive from Sunset Crater, stands on a rocky outcropping facing the Painted Desert.

V · THE EAST

In the country that lies east of the Great Plains are national parks on a piece of the granite coast of Maine, a great wilderness island in Lake Superior, a tropical waterfowl refuge in Florida, a venerable cave in Kentucky, forested mountain ranges blue with mist, and a stark and dazzling stretch of beach. They are all peaceable places, well watered and well mannered. These are places that replenish and fulfill the spirit, rather than dazzle the eye.

Everglades National Park FLORIDA

Everglades National Park, which occupies the southern end of Florida including the many islets of Florida Bay, is the odd child of our family of national parks. It is both Congo and Amazon and it also has hints of the South Pacific. But it is not quite a jungle while it is surely not typical of a temperate zone swamp.

It occasionally gets frosts, but most years it is warm, often swelteringly hot. Its plants and animals show the nature of its extremes. The pond-cypress trees everywhere in it are deciduous, shedding their leaves seasonally just as trees do in the northern regions.

In addition to rabbits, raccoons, wildcats, otters, bear, deer and panthers (or "painters," as they are still called by some native Floridians), the Everglades Park is the home of alligators, crocodiles, and manatees.

Its most colorful inhabitants are birds. Roseate spoonbills, white ibis with black-tipped wings and red bills, pelicans, both white and brown, reddish egrets, yellow-crowned night heron (called a "squawk" by oldtimers), purple gallinule—these are foremost among the many species that make up the spectrum of its birdlife.

Great white herons eat small fish. Like most other Everglades birds, they migrate north in the summer.

Unique to the Everglades are its great reptiles. Thirty years ago, it wasn't unusual to see newly hatched alligators crawling thickly over raised clearings in the marshes and along streamshores. They were gathered by the bushel to be sold in shops, and were mailed alive as souvenirs to all parts of the country.

Today, by law, they can't be either gathered or sold. What are now displayed as alligators by Florida's curio sellers are actually cousins, young caymans, shipped up from South America.

There are only two species of alligators in the world, the American and a smaller variety in China. Both are members of the crocodile family, which numbers about fourteen species. An alligator has a wide head without the exposed fourth side tooth of the slimmer-headed crocodile. The relatively rare American crocodile lives mostly

Roseate spoonbills like to congregate. Plume hunters almost exterminated these magnificent birds.

in the swamp's salt-water areas while the alligato
stays primarily in fresh water.

Alligators can be dangerous—in the past, 19-
footers were known. But they aren't regarded a
harmful predators: their diet consists mainly o
turtles and garfish.

By contrast, the swamp's big water mammal
the torpid manatee, is about as harmless as
large animal can be. More closely related t
elephants than to whales, the manatee spends it
life browsing on underwater plants; and abou
the only thing that might excite one would be
fish that accidentally wandered into its mouth

The legend of mermaids is said to have sprun
from the spectacle of a manatee nursing he
young. But it's an odd explanation considerin

*A small alligator suns himself on a rock. Hunters kille
many of his kind, but those living in the park are safe*

An air boat is pushed by an airplane propellor and skims across the shallows. Clumps far off in distance are called hammocks.

that these ugly, mustached beasts often weigh around a thousand pounds.

Another sight in the Everglades is an occasional Seminole Indian. The aboriginal Calusas have long since gone, leaving little trace of their ancient ways. But the later-coming Seminoles are sometimes about, poling their slim dugouts through the sawgrass water-prairies usually along the Tamiami trail which parallels a portion of the northern boundary of the park.

In the western region, great, impenetrable mangrove thickets bar travel off the waterways; but in the north, sawgrass marshes are the park's chief scenic wonders. They extend for miles, dotted by hammocks crowded with palms. These raised-soil islands vary from lot-size to a few acres.

Here—where Indians hunted—white men now cruise in amphibious "swamp buggies," which both roll and float on overlarge tires; and also in shallow boats driven by air propellers. Such rides can be hired at several places around the park's edges although use of them is not permitted in the park itself.

But there are also waterways solidly choked by water hyacinth—prolific plants brought to this country from South America more than a generation ago. The story goes that a Florida housewife threw the excess from her garden pond into the nearest stream. Since then the plants have invaded nearly every waterway in the state, clogging navigation and fishing areas and posing a great problem for both state and national governments.

Their lavender bloom is small compensation. Anyway, before they arrived there was color enough for the most hungry eye—in the ground orchids and bluehearts of the piney woods, in the tree orchids of the hammocks, and in the scarlet coral beans of everywhere.

Eden-like though it may seem, the park in summer is plagued by mosquitoes, which dominate whole areas to the extent that exploration of the nature trails is only for the hardy. Winter is best for sightseeing, when there are fewer mosquitoes and moderate weather makes travel pleasanter.

Birds and animals may also be quieter then, and there is less of the jungle-like odor of plants

A cruiser explores a large drainage canal. Excessive drainage has dried out large areas creating serious fire hazards throughout the swamp.

A Seminole poles his dugout canoe. Indians do not live in the park, but their settlements dot the nearby areas. Below, *two women stand in typical native dress.*

decomposing in water. But enough of both sound and aroma remain to remind you that life teems in Everglades National Park.

If you travel by car, you can reach Everglades by taking U.S. 1 out of Miami, then State Highway 27 south from Florida City.

The main Visitor Center is located just inside the park and an orientation stop here is advisable. Two miles beyond, a spur road leads to the Royal Palm area where another visitor center is the hub of the Anhinga (elevated) Trail and the Gumbo Limbo Trail. There are regularly scheduled ranger-naturalist programs and conducted hikes.

State Road 27 and the main park road join at the park boundary and continue on for 38 miles to Flamingo. Daily ranger-naturalist programs of talks and conducted walks are available here. Boat tours of various types are concession-operated. Modern motel, marina, and dining room and coffee shop facilities are open all year.

Into the park's waters come jewfish, tarpon, dolphin and other gamefish. At Cape Sable, the tip of Florida, sea trout, redfish, snook, snapper and grouper are common in the shallows. Information on the necessary tackle and bait, and on the fishing laws, may be had at any of the many bait and tackle stores on the roads leading to the park, and at Flamingo.

Ranger-conducted boat trips are scheduled on Saturdays during the winter months at Flamingo and at Everglades City, the western water gateway to the park. Everglades City is just four miles off U.S. 41 on State Road 29. Boat and fishing tours and all supplies are available here to visitors.

Everglades National Park

S Florida. Area: 2,188 sq. mi.
Season: year round.
Climate: summers hot and humid.
Accommodations: many motels in the area, trailer space.
Services: museum, boat rentals, fishing, hunting.
US highways 1, 27, and 41, lead to park.

Shenandoah valley, dimmed by mist, lies just west of the oak-forested Blue Ridge range.

Shenandoah National Park VIRGINIA

Virginia's Blue Ridge Mountains, the showpiece of Shenandoah National Park, have little use for superlatives. They simply combine calm beauty with easy accessibility. Half the people in the United States can reach the park overnight. When they come, they're not looking for the most stupendous or, the most exciting park—but for the quietest, the most restful, the easiest on the nerves.

The mountains have more important qualities than height. Gifts of nature lie strewn around in such profusion that these 330 square miles add up to a superlative after all. They constitute the eastern taxpayer's biggest bargain—a cool, forested, often misty upland of greenery rising from the workaday sea-level world.

And best of all, near the crest of the long, leafy mountain range runs an easy-going highway in the sky that puts the visitor within a short walk of almost every attraction in the narrow park. From Front Royal to Rockfish Gap the Skyline Drive meanders 105 amiable miles, pausing for 75 eye-resting overlooks. Stop for a picnic, then go for a hike to a rounded mountain peak or a wispy waterfall.

You can enjoy Shenandoah without hiking, but since walking in the woods is one of the best ways to escape civilization, you shouldn't fail to try it. Take your choice of 203 miles of paths, including a 94-mile stretch of the Appalachian Trail which runs—or rather walks—from Maine to Georgia.

Tiny Dutchman's britches prefer deep shade in the woods. Eighty varieties of flowers grow in the Park.

Turk's-cap lily likes a warm climate best. These large, showy plants thrive in the low-lying, open meadows.

You'll probably prefer to strike out on your own on the shorter, self-guiding trails. But most popular are the many walks led by ranger-naturalists. Hikes range from 1.5 to 5 miles (round trip). Two favorites reach Whiteoak Canyon's waterfalls and Stony Man's stunted-oak forehead and greenstone nose, which will bring you 4,010 feet above sea level.

During the summer months, nightly campfire programs are given on a wide variety of natural history subjects by the range naturalists. In spring and fall, similar talks are presented by Park Naturalists at the concession lodges.

Every visitor to a National Park should inquire about visitor centers. By means of exhibits and short orientation programs, these centers acquaint visitors with the major Park features and suggest what to see and do. Dicky Ridge Visitor Center is 4.6 miles south of the north entrance to Shenandoah via the Skyline Drive, at the southern edge of Front Royal, Virginia.

Pick up the weekly schedule of the visitor activities at the visitor centers or developed areas. For more extensive walking, buy the topographic maps of the Potomac Appalachian Trail Club and choose among 20 circuit hikes. Overnight hikers can reserve equipped cabins by writing the club's headquarters, 1916 Sunderland Place, N. W., Washington 6, D. C. The Park Service itself maintains 20 open shelters (no bedding supplied), each one sleeping six persons, and is shared on a first-come, first-served basis.

Most satisfactory hike from a "job well done" point of view is the Old Rag Mountain circuit. You start from the bottom, near Nethers, Virginia, and climb the Ridge Trail to the rocky "raggedy" top (3,291 feet), then descend via the Saddle Trail and Weakley Hollow Fire Road. It's a good day's work (about 8 miles altogether), but there are two shelters nearby if you want to stay overnight.

If you want something faster than shank's mare, but less powerful than your 200-horsepower car, you might settle for a one-horsepower horse. You can rent one by the hour at Skyland or Big Meadows and ride along 25 miles of bridle paths.

Chances are that most of the things you'll do

in Shenandoah will center around Skyland, Big Meadows, or Lewis Mountain, the three lodges in the central section. Skyland, highest point on Skyline Drive, is the birthplace of the park. There, at 3,680 feet, George Freeman Pollock built a remote mountain hideaway in 1898. Were he to come back today, he'd have the company of 300 daily lodgers, several hundred diners, and a thousand or so passers-through. The dining room hangs on the lip of a cliff and looks directly down on tic-tac-toe streets of Luray, Virginia, almost 3,000 feet below. Raise the eyes slightly and you're looking into Massanutten, a blockish mountain dropped almost whimsically into the middle of Shenandoah Valley.

Big Meadows has everything Skyland does, plus an enormous camping area. Big as it is, it's wise to arrive early for assigned camping spaces, especially on weekends. There is no charge for camping, other than the 50c daily or $1.00 yearly admission fee to the park itself. In 1961 the total annual camping days allowed was lowered to 14. Reservations for cabins or rooms in all three centers can be made (April through November) by writing Virginia Skyland Co., Luray, Virginia.

This company operates restaurants also at Thornton Gap (Panorama) (open all year) and Swift Run Gap, two passes where major highways cross Skyline Drive. Other entrances to the park are at Front Royal (northern end) and Rockfish Gap (southern end) where Skyline Drive becomes the Blue Ridge Parkway and plunges another 469 miles through the Southern Appalachians.

These mountains were the first barrier Americans crossed in their march from Atlantic to Pacific. They are held in fond nostalgia by a nation remembering its youth of coonskin caps, log cabins, trail-breaking, and square dancing to a one-string fiddle.

The cabins are gone; the few that remained when the park took shape in the early '30's are decaying. But sometimes, deep on the trail, the smell of apple blossoms wafts through. You break into a silent clearing of seedling apples and know that here a frontier axe once rang. Here a cabin rose among the oaks, chestnuts, and dogwood "fur enough that I cain't see the chimney smoke over to Nicholson Holler."

Shenandoah National Park

Central Virginia. Area: 330 sq. mi.
Season: year round. April-Oct. best.
Climate: mild to warm in summer.
Accommodations: lodges, motels, trailer sites.
Services: visitor centers, campfire programs, shops, restaurants, garages.
Buses, trains, US highway 340 from Front Royal or Charlottesville all lead to park.

Clintonia, sometimes called bear tongue, lives in rich, moist, woodland soils where there is plenty of shade.

Snowy trillium grows in the deep woods. A member of the lily family, it grows about eight inches tall.

Great Smoky Mountains National Park NORTH CAROLINA

The trees help to make the mist that gives the mountains their name.

These rolling peaks are so heavily wooded that droplets of vapor given off from the leaves cloud the air. This is the smoke of the Smokies and the blue of the Blue Ridge to the north.

To preserve a portion of this woodland, Great Smoky Mountains National Park was formed—an 800-square-mile preserve, the largest stand of virgin hardwood forests in eastern North America. In doing so its creators also managed to establish the most popular park in the system. More people come here than to any other national park.

Although far and away the most looked-at park, the Smokies may also qualify as the least seen. Most visitors seem tied by some invisible chain to their cars—and the Smokies are a walker's paradise.

The Smokies abound in swift-running streams.

True, you can have a good time by car—millions do. But to really see the park you must get out and walk. There are trails to suit every taste. Some are four feet wide with an easy gradient. Some are improved footpaths. Others are merely tracks through the forest. Altogether they total some 600 miles. And if you want to hike instead of walk, try the Appalachian Trail. The mile-high ridge of the Smokies winds for 68 miles through the park and the trail follows it most of the way. You can start at the dam on Fontana Lake, at one end. Or you can take off at the middle where U.S. 441 crosses Newfound Gap. Going east from this point, the trail passes through 31 miles of virgin wilderness. You can camp for the night at any of thirteen shelters. But you must have a permit for trail camping. Rangers at park headquarters or any ranger station will cheerfully provide one.

For a good introduction to the park, join a group led by a park naturalist (there are scheduled walks each day from spring through fall) and you will discover a strange thing:

The Smokies are southern—but northern at the same time. If you scattered 500,000 acres of New England along the North Carolina-Tennessee border, you'd have something like the Smokies. On top of these mist-shrouded peaks you'll find trees, birds, insects, and temperatures typical of country 1,000 miles north.

In part, this accounts for their popularity. Unlike the western parks, the Smokies are surrounded by areas of heavy population. Many people from Knoxville, Tennessee, and Asheville, North Carolina, drive over just to get the coolness of a summer's day. You can see them sitting beside their cars on the high mountain overlooks, overlooking the scenery. They've seen it all before, and seem bored. Boredom is hard to maintain, however. Even those who have lived all their lives in this section find delight here. Some

Hikers inspect Alum Cave, a favorite stopover on the ten-mile round trip hike up Mount Le Compte.

come each weekend, and they will tell you they find new pleasure every time.

What do they come to see? The mountains, of course, sixteen of them rising above 6,000 feet. They fill the horizon in all directions, as green as they were when Columbus changed the world's idea of itself.

The Smokies are steep, but they are not pinnacles and rock faces like the upstart Tetons in the West, a mere million years old. They are soft and sloping, in the calm graciousness of maturity. They are among the most ancient mountains on earth. That the Smokies are here at all is amazing, for they began their rise some 300 million years before the Tetons. One rocky thumb still sticks up. But it too will be smoothed off before long, in terms of mountains.

On the state line stands Charlie's Bunion, named for a sore-footed guide. It is bare because a forest fire killed the trees. Then heavy rain washed off the soil. But plants are beginning to cover it again. First came the lichens and mosses, etching the rock, making a little soil for the ferns, blackberries, rhododendron and others to root in. As these grow, they'll slowly build the earth covering needed for balsam fir and red spruce. Then Charlie's Bunion may again be as wooded as other peaks. Meantime, there are several other peaks just as bare. They are called balds, and nobody really minds for after a hard walk you can stand on one of them and see the forest instead of just the trees.

From Gatlinburg, Tennessee, on the north edge of the park, or from Cherokee, North Carolina, on the south, a few minutes by car or a few hours by foot will take you out of the south's heat into the cool climate of Canada. You won't be the first to discover this; some lazy birds beat you to it. For centuries they have been migrating—not the long miles from south to north, but the few thousand feet from the base to the mountain tops.

When the rains come—and they often do—they swell some of the most beautiful streams in the world. A total of 600 miles of them lace the park. On every mountain flank, in every valley, there is water as good as you will ever taste. Cold, clear, sparkling, rushing downhill, these streams are pure unless otherwise marked.

Ramsey Cascades are largest in the park. A trail starts at Greebriar Cove, 11 miles from Gatlinburg.

The larger streams have many trout. A system called "fishing for fun" is in effect on several. This is a fly fisherman's dream come true. You can catch as many fish as your skill allows—and you can catch them at any time of the year. But you must put them back into the water unharmed (except for trophy fish 16 or more inches long). For a fellow who likes to fish, but hates to clean and cook the catch, this is ideal. On other streams the regular park fishing regulations pertain.

For some visitors, the trees, the flowers, and the peaks are not the chief attraction, although they were the reason the park was created. The real lure is a shaggy, flat-footed beggar who earns his dinner simply by making the scene.

He is, of course, a bear. Bears patrol the roadsides, searching for leftovers from picnics or anything else edible. It is unlawful to throw Bruin a hot dog or candy bar in order to photograph him. As the signs will inform you, bears are wild animals, and not to be trusted. Don't get too close, and don't tease. Every year several people are hauled off to the hospital in Gatlinburg to recover from a clawed slap. (Hint: if you want detail in your bear pictures, open the camera diaphragm an extra stop.)

Most bears are found on the Tennessee side of the road that bisects the park (Route 441). On this side, a spur road leads to Cades Cove.

Here you see the way a self-sufficient people lived when the country was young. The cove is a wide and fertile cup in the mountains that, before 1933 when the park was created, held a complete community.

In those days, Cades Cove needed little from the outside. It had its own churches, its own distillery. It grew its own grain and meat, had its own flour mill.

World War I was the first strong outside influence; many of the boys went off to fight—and saw the world. The first good road came in in 1926.

Today the Cove boasts a one-way road. Looping around it, this road carries you to pioneer cabins and a working gristmill. Churches are

Rhododendron is one of the most dazzling flowering shrubs in the States. Rose-purple flowers bloom in June.

flanked by the weathered slates that marked graves in the days when each family kept its coffin wood set aside in the barn. The coffin makers worked to personal measurements, all night if need be, until the box was finished.

To keep the cove floor open so visitors can see the ringing mountains, the Park Service permits farmers to work certain fields—carefully selected by the park architect. Some of the "permitees" are members of the old families that settled the cove; some are newcomers.

After Congress created the Great Smoky Mountains National Park, it was decided that there would be no concessions inside. So the hotels, motels, restaurants and the like are all on the borders—except one that predates the park.

On top of Old Smoky (whatever mountain is nearest is given that name)—well, then, on top of Mount Le Comte is a "lodge." This is a kind of hotel in the clouds. Its water supply is a cold spring; its heating a series of fireplaces. Its menu is whatever the proprietors have decided to cook for dinner that night. For reservations, write Herrick Brown, Gatlinburg, Tennessee.

You can get there only by foot or horseback. The entertainment is the mountain scenery, especially the sunrise and sunset, which are superb. Some people, however, pray for rain at sunrise so they can enjoy their bunks a bit longer.

For more ordinary accommodations write the Chambers of Commerce at Gatlinburg, Townsend, Knoxville, and Maryville, Tennessee; Asheville, Waynesville, Bryson City, Cherokee, and Silva, North Carolina. Auto campers have a choice of six campgrounds, modern but without electricity. Inquire at the park headquarters.

Most visitors to the Smokies spend a day or two at the Cherokee Indian Reservation, which adjoins the park where U.S. 19 comes in from Asheville. On the reservation are shops, restaurants, an exhibition village and the pageant "Unto These Hills." Recently, modern motels and other facilities have been constructed.

The terrible blot in the history of these mountains is the shameful treatment of the Cherokee by the United States over 100 years ago. But today we all can be proud of the preservation of the extraordinary natural beauty of the Smokies.

Great Smoky Mountains National Park

North Carolina-Tennessee. Area: 798 sq. mi.

Season: year round.

Climate: warm summers, milder in winter, summits always cooler; autumn least foggy and rainy

Accommodations: lodge, camp and trailer sites, hotels and motels nearby.

US 441 from Knoxville to Ashville, Tenn. approaches park.

A hardy breed of mountaineer lived isolated in the Smokies until the 1940's. Here is a typical cabin.

Six hundred and fifty miles of trails await hikers. Some are just paths. Others, like this one, are four feet wide.

Isle Royale National Park

LAKE SUPERIOR

Two hundred wooded islets cluster near the main island in the western section of Lake Superior.

Once there was the great North Woods. This broad belt of wilderness covered the north-central United States, the domain of moose, wolves, beaver, Indians, and a few lonely French trappers. It was the setting for the legends of Paul Bunyan. Then the land was tamed and cultivated. The legends were driven out, and towns and cities rose. The North Woods dwindled away except for one remnant. That is Isle Royale, a wilderness island in the western waters of Lake Superior, where the Park Service guards it from the pressure of civilization.

Isle Royale National Park includes a big island, 45 miles long and nine miles wide, and about 200 islets scattered in an archipelago and giving a total of over 800 square miles of park area. Even on the large island no vehicles are allowed. You must explore the great forest on foot.

Here live timber wolves and moose in a naturally balanced scheme of wildlife. Here rule the laws of nature, free from the tampering of man.

Too often men try mistakenly to make life easier for animals such as deer by getting rid of the meat-eaters–wolves, mountain lions, bears, coyotes, and foxes. Then comes trouble. Deer herds grow too big for their grazing region. There isn't enough food to go around. The region is stripped bare. Even in our national parks a good deal of grass and trees has been destroyed beyond recovery because conservationists have killed wolves, for example, without regard for their place in nature's plan.

But on Isle Royale, moose are thriving. They are a common sight near the water, lipping weeds from the shore, squishing through mud. There are just enough of them to prosper–thanks to the wolves that prey on unfit calves and old, sick ones. And the flora of the park is rich and abundant. Nature is in balance.

Isle Royale's moose probably migrated to the island during the great freeze of 1912, when Lake Superior froze over. Beaver, muskrat, mink, weasel, coyote, fox, hare, and squirrel made the trip long ago, after the last glacier melted away. Deer, porcupine, and skunk, however are not found in the park.

Neither, thankfully, is poison ivy. The park's plants include 36 kinds of orchid and many flowers native to the North Woods. Botanists are surprised to find devil's club growing here. It belongs in the Pacific Northwest and isn't found elsewhere in the Great Lakes region. As you roam the woods, watch for the Indianpipe or ghostflower. It is colorless and leafless, a holdover from far back in plant history before the development of chlorophyll-colored vegetation.

Trees of two weather zones grow in the park. Sugar maples and yellow birches, common in the northern states, share the forest with the balsams, spruces, poplars, and white birches, that are typical of Canadian forests.

Wild as the island is, it was the scene of extensive mining by prehistoric Indians. They worked its copper deposits for centuries, stripping nuggets from pits and trading them in one form or another over a great part of the continent. Isle Royale's copper may even have been worked before prehistoric Britain's mines were being dug.

French explorers named the island in honor of Louis XIV when France took possession of it in 1671. As the fabulous voyagers opened the Northwest to the fur trade, they paddled past the island on their way to the Grand Portage route. The beginning of that route is about 20 miles to the west, at Grand Portage, Minnesota.

In 1763, after the defeat of the French in the

French and Indian War, the British claimed the island. In 1783 the island was ceded to the United States by the Peace of Paris treaty. However, the area remained essentially British until after the War of 1812. In 1843 the Chippewa tribe relinquished their last claim on the island. After 1899 mining interests largely abandoned the island, leaving only commercial fishermen and a few small resort operators interested in the island.

The island lies closer to Canada than to the United States. It's about a dozen miles off the Ontario shore. Only a boat or seaplane will get you there. An outboard is about the best way of getting around it unless you are experienced in rugged woodland hiking. Boat service is available at Houghton and Copper Harbor, Michigan, and Grand Portage, Minnesota.

The inland lakes of Isle Royale have many game fish—pike, perch, walleyes, brook and lake trout. Whitefish and cisco can be caught here, too. Shores and harbors of the island also offer fine fishing for brook and rainbow trout and northern pike. If your fishing is done within the Park boundaries, which extend four and a half miles from the main island out into Lake Superior, a fishing license is not required.

Boats, guides, and fishing tackle are available at Rock Harbor, on the eastern end of the island, or at Windigo, at the western end. You must bring your own outboard if you don't like rowing or paddling. Rock Harbor offers lodging, as does the Windigo Inn. Write for rates and make your reservations beforehand. Campers should bring adequate equipment and supplies, but some can be bought at either lodge.

If you plan a visit, get ready for a cool climate—even at the height of summer. Wear sturdy boots or shoes. And one aid to comfort—just as important here as it is at the other end of the country in the Everglades—is mosquito repellent.

Isle Royale National Park

Michigan, northern Lake Superior. Area: 210 sq. mi.
Season: summer months (June 25-Labor Day).
Climate: cool days, cold nights.
Accommodations: camp sites, lodgings.
Services: boat rentals, fishing.
Can be reached only by seaplane or boat, from Houghton and Copper Harbor, Mich., or Grand Portage, Minn., or Ontario.

Fishermen must paddle to reach the big game fish in Isle Royale's 30 lakes. No motors are allowed.

Acadia National Park MAINE

Writers exclaim over the coast of Maine so often that their descriptions lose meaning. "Rugged," "rockbound," and "pine-clad" generally fail to stir up any visions of this northeastern shore. Yet the Maine coast is all of them and much more, too. It is a splendid part of the country—shaped and hammered by vast natural forces, softened by forests, haunted by human history. People cannot visit these coves and harbors without falling hopelessly in love with the feeling of morning fog burning off under a warm sun, the scent of pine needles in the cool shade of the forest, the taste of wild blueberries, the muffled thunder of waves, the crisp hue of sunset on a cool evening. And the best example of the 3,478-mile Maine coast (including the islands) is Acadia National Park, which became the first great park in the East.

During the last Ice Age, this shoreline was pressed down by the huge weight of ice and snow. Glaciers scraped the rocky land, smoothed the hills, cracked loose rock away from parent ledges. The result is a sunken coast where what were once valleys are now sounds and inlets, where little granite islands jut from the ocean, where tumbled boulders clog the shore. Most of Maine is like this; Acadia typifies it. For here rise the heights of Mount Desert Island, the round-sculptured remnants of a pre-Ice Age mountain ridge. Its tallest summit is still the highest point in the United States that overlooks the Atlantic, and one of the first to catch the rising sun's rays.

A deep, narrow sound cuts Mount Desert Island almost in two: Somes Sound, the only true fjord on the New England coast. On either side the hills rise, covered with tough, stunted pine and spruce—and some not so stunted—and rich with wildflowers. Cadillac Mountain, 1,530 feet, marks the high point. Below it spreads Frenchman Bay and the old, wealthy summer resort of Bar Harbor.

Acadia was donated to the Federal government by the summer residents (once called "rusticaters" by the locals) who, between them, owned most of Mount Desert Island. That's why the park boundaries are strangely uneven—they follow property lines. Most of the 48-square-mile park lies on Mount Desert Island; some is across Frenchman Bay on Schoodic Peninsula; some occupies part of Isle au Haut, an offshore island southwest of Mount Desert. All these park lands contain choice elements of scenery. Fresh-water ponds and lakes gleam among the dark evergreens on Mount Desert. Trout, salmon, and bass flirt with the angler, while salt-water fishing invites visitors to brave the gray Atlantic in chartered vessels.

Miles of trails lead to the hilltops and vantage points of Mount Desert. And carriage roads—holdovers from the gracious old days of great estates—are kept especially for horseback riding. Surfaced roads link mountains with shore. The highway up Cadillac Mountain is called the best-engineered mountain road in the world, never steeper than an easy seven percent gradient. Two free campgrounds welcome visitors who come to Mount Desert.

A fine road loops around the Schoodic Peninsula and reaches out to Schoodic Point, where the whole Atlantic comes rolling and crashing in a brilliant display of power after a storm. Isle au Haut is the park's wilderness area, isolated and beautiful. You can get there by ferry, but you can't take your car. There are no accommodations, not even campsites or picnic facilities. The only sign of civilization in the park section of Isle au Haut is a rustic road leading past spruce forests and around the balding hills that rise above the sea and offer a sparkling view of it.

At Acadia there is an interplay of ocean and forest life. Tiny coralline algae line the pools of water with an enamel-like rose coloring in Anemone Cave while white-tail deer wander within sight of the salt spray on summer evenings. Beaver slosh busily about the hidden fresh-water ponds while big mottled green lobsters lie on the deep ocean bottom.

Atlantic swells surge and crash on the granite of Acadia near Thunder Hole. Seals often play close by the rocks.

Human beings, too, add to the significance of Acadia. Its name suggests the French settlers of colonial days who constantly fought with the English about who owned what inlet along the Maine coast. Champlain found and named the "Isle des Monts Deserts" (Island of Barren Mountains), and Sieur de la Mothe Cadillac, later founder of Detroit and governor of Louisiana, took it over as his feudal domain until the English won all of eastern America. Cadillac's descendants pressed the family claim after the Revolution, but Mount Desert Island seemed more a white elephant than a precious legacy until summer people discovered it a few years before the Civil War.

Summer people still flock to Bar Harbor, often driving cars named for the region's colonial lord. And the year-rounders still buck the foggy seas to catch lobster as they have for generations. Things change slowly down in Maine, and around Acadia National Park change is one thing you don't look for.

Acadia National Park

NE Maine. Area: 48 sq. mi.
Season: June-Sept.
Climate: cool.
Accommodations: camp sites, summer lodgings.
Services: boating, fishing, hunting; naturalist service.
Highways, air and rail travel and ferries go to park.

Cape Hatteras National Seashore Recreational Area

NORTH CAROLINA

On the map of the eastern seaboard, a long, slender wisp of land lies off the shoreline of North Carolina. Channels cut it in places, turning it into a series of thin islands, the Outer Banks.

Here Sir Walter Raleigh founded the first English colony in America, the ill-fated settlement at Roanoke Island. Here Blackbeard the Pirate prowled. Here the Wright brothers tried out their flying machine. And here the Park Service set up its first national seashore recreation area along an 80-mile stretch of the banks that includes famous Cape Hatteras.

From the north, you drive across one of two long bridges that link the banks to the mainland. U.S. Route 158 crosses Currituck Sound and deposits you at Kitty Hawk, close to the sandy Kill Devil Hill where the Wright Brothers National Memorial stands. Here the Wrights' plane reeled off the ground for 12 glorious seconds on a bitter December day in 1903. One reason the Wrights chose the place was its steady breeze. You feel it as you take to the highway that splits the banks. There are no gusts, no sudden calms, just a constant push of air such as you'd expect on a ship.

Driving south on the banks you pass the resort town of Nags Head. U.S. Route 64 joins you here after crossing from the mainland by way of Roanoke Island and Fort Raleigh National Historic Site. The banks highway now enters the Park Service domain and a pause at the visitor center near Coquina Beach is worth your time.

You are entering a remote world of sand, sun, wind, and waves. It is not crowded. Traffic is light. Campgrounds are beautifully maintained and always seem to have room for a few more. Long, long beaches stretch to the horizon with only a random scattering of bathers and surf casters. The fishing is marvelous: bluefish darting through the surf get uncontrollably hungry on the spur of the moment and will snap at even the badly flung bait of the clumsiest amateur.

A bridge from the mainland is under construc-

Seventy miles of uncrowded beach stretch from Nag's Head to Ocracoke Inlet. Surfing's fine but shade is rare.

tion at Oregon Inlet and will be opened to traffic in late 1963. Until then, the free ferry across Oregon Inlet is the only means of transportation to the 50-mile stretch of Hatteras Island. You will be cut off from the rest of the United States by the 30-mile-wide shoal waters of Pamlico Sound. You are also at the mercy of the weather. To some, the isolation is unsettling. But to most, there is a tingle of excitement as they rumble onto the ferry and head toward the empty dunes.

A few villages and settlements offer food and lodging on Hatteras Island. But the campground at Cape Hatteras is sizable and a good central point from which to explore the banks. Nearby is Cape Hatteras Lighthouse, the tallest in the United States, and for the youthful and determined a climb to its gallery is worth the 268 steps. You look down and out at some 20 miles of shoreline. To your left it runs almost due north. Just to the south is the small rounded point that marks the apex of the cape. And there the Outer Banks make a near 90-degree turn, running almost west. Here flow the offshoots of the Gulf Stream, bringing warm water to wash the southern banks. But off the point they meet the south-flowing waters of the Labrador Current, where they drop the swirling sands they carry.

Thus Diamond Shoals are formed, and when the sea runs high surf crashes mightily on them and sends the spume rocketing. Any ship that drifts too close is done for. Some 600 have struck along the banks and pounded themselves to pieces, so that Cape Hatteras is known as "Graveyard of the Atlantic." Among its wrecks is the famed USS *Monitor* which sank in a gale while being towed past the cape. The most mysterious relic, however, is the bow of the *Carroll A. Deering*. A five-masted schooner, the *Deering* struck Diamond Shoals in 1921. Rescuers found only the ship's cat aboard, though a meal was ready for serving in the galley. Winter storms broke the ship up; its bow fetched on Ocracoke Island where it still crops up out of the drifting sand every so often, then vanishes again.

Another ferry takes you to Ocracoke Island, a wild ribbon of dunes barren of all villages except picturesque Ocracoke at the western end. As you drive down the island, watch for wild horses. Lately the rangers have corralled them because they harmed the vegetation that keeps this sandy soil from blowing away.

A hermit crab finds a home in a moon snail shell.

The town of Ocracoke, set around its nearly landlocked harbor, seems like a Cape Cod village gone astray—the same small, weatherbeaten cottages and clean little churches and general stores. This was the realm of Blackbeard, Edward Teach, whose success as a pirate was notorious.

Ocracoke has another campground and the same fine fishing and swimming as Hatteras. It is possible, though expensive, to drive aboard another ferry at Ocracoke Inlet and make a long trip to Atlantic on the North Carolina mainland.

Life abounds along the national seashore. Rangers show how to catch various crabs, how to tell one shell from another. Porpoises leap just off the beach. Charter fishermen—"bankers" with a curiously English accent—take parties out through the inlets and often bring back marlin and sailfish. A group of visitors is always waiting at the docks to see the boats return and to spot the sailfish pennant telling of good luck.

Days pass quickly at Cape Hatteras. Perhaps too quickly if a hurricane happens to swing toward that frail barrier of sand. Then the rangers awaken campers and lodgers and send them flying for ferries and bridges.

Cape Hatteras National Seashore Recreational Area

E North Carolina. Area: 80 mi. strip.

Season: year round.

Climate: warm seashore.

Accommodations: limited lodgings, campgrounds.

Services: stores, restaurants, museum, visitor centers, beach shelters. Fishing, boat rental, hunting.

Bus from Norfolk, other highways to free ferry at Oregon Inlet lead to Hatteras Island.

Mammoth Cave National Park KENTUCKY

During the War of 1812, the young and struggling United States found itself cut off from materials for making gunpowder. Then it was discovered that the dry dirt in some caves contained all-important saltpeter. As a result, in one day Mammoth Cave was sold several times, first for $116.67, and last for $3,000. A month later, part interest went for $10,000.

Ever since then, Mammoth Cave has been famous. A hundred years ago no man could say he knew his country who had not seen Niagara Falls and Mammoth Cave, "the greatest cave there ever was." They came by horse, stagecoach, and later by rail to Cave City, nearby. The Emperor of Brazil came, and Grand Duke Alexis of Imperial Russia: Jenny Lind gave a concert in the cave, and a throng of visitors stood in awe as the walls rang to her golden voice. Edwin Booth recited Hamlet's gloomy philosophy from a natural pedestal underground. Outlaws also took interest. Jesse James once held up the Mammoth Cave stage and relieved its passengers of $831 and a gold watch.

Today you can mount wooden stairs and stand where Booth stood, and look down on Booth's Amphitheater. Nearby you can see a stretch of wooden pipes. These are bored-out tree trunks, laid to carry saltpeter solution to the boiling vats outside. The dry cave air, at a constant 54 degrees, has preserved the wood perfectly for 150 years. You can also see Mummy John, the dry and preserved corpse of an Indian killed centuries ago by a falling rock.

This historic cave is the chief attraction of Mammoth Cave National Park, an 80-square-mile preserve in west-central Kentucky. It lies a hundred miles south of Louisville, and the same distance north of Nashville, Tennessee. Unlike New Mexico's Carlsbad Caverns, which is a series of huge rooms, Mammoth is a web of corridors, interspersed with vast domes that reach almost to the surface, and deep, plunging pits. The passages are ancient underground river channels. So far, 150 miles have been explored. The rock in this part of the country is flat-bed limestone, laid down some 200,000,000 years ago in the bed of a primordial sea. The land rose and surface water seeped into the ground and found its way along hard beds of rock. As the millions of years went by, the streams grew and ate away at the rock, until today the passageways are 50 feet high in places, and as wide as 200 feet. The land continued to rise. The rivers cut new channels at lower levels. Today, most of the cave is dry, but at the lowest level, you can walk along the dark shores of the River Styx, which still flows 300 feet below the ground. In another section you can take a boat ride on Echo River.

There are five cave tours, ranging from the seven-and-half-mile All Day Trip, to the short Frozen Niagara Trip. No visitors are allowed in the cave without a guide. Mammoth Cave is no place to seek adventure. It has been in business too long, and all the tours are run on schedule and lighted by electricity. However, part of its charm is the salty character of the park guides. Some of them are third or fourth generation cave guides; their fathers and grandfathers were lifelong guides before them.

What you will see in the cave can best be described by the names of some of the formations: Fat Man's Misery, a narrow squiggle of a channel cut into the floor of a large chamber, Grand Central Station, Giant's Coffin, Ruins of Karnak, Frozen Niagara, Grand Canyon, Crystal Lake, The visitor center at the park headquarters contains a large, lighted map. A visit will help you decide just what you would like to see.

Although the cave trips are the main thing, there is plenty to do above ground. A total of 30 miles of river (the Green and the Nolin) flows through the park. Fishing is allowed, and no license is required, but fishermen should stop at park headquarters and ask about park regulations.

An excursion boat will take you on a one and a half-hour trip down the lovely Green River. It leaves five times daily during summer from Mammoth Cave Ferry. Eight miles of trail lead through the dense woods along the river bank. The forest is at its best during fall when leaves turn fiery red and orange.

The woods are really quite lovely as they are, but eventually, in another generation or so, they will have grown again to their natural state. Then an 80-square-mile forest wilderness will stand again, towering and superb—a sample of what the whole eastern part of America looked like before all the land was cleared by white men.

Overnight lodging is available at Mammoth Cave Hotel (write National Park Concessions, Inc., Mammoth Cave, Ky.). A half mile away are modern camp and trailer grounds.

Mammoth Cave National Park

Central Kentucky. Area: 51,000 acres, 150 mi. of explored passages.

Season: year round.

Climate: mild.

Accommodations: lodging available, camp and trailer sites nearby.

Services: guided tours, visitor center, fishing.

Cave is 10 mi. west of Cave City on State Highway 70.

Echo River, at lowest level, lies 360 feet below ground. The rest of the cave is dry, and walking is the thing.

VI · OUTLYING PARKS

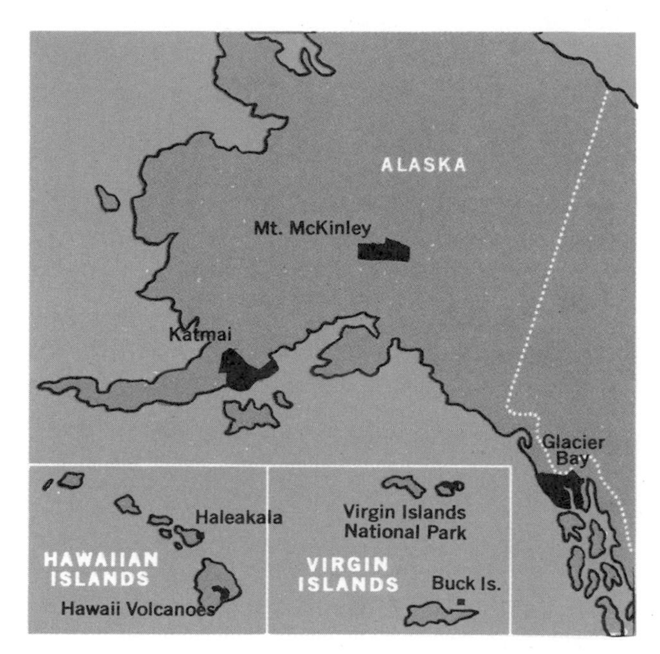

The great park areas of Alaska are untouched wildernesses, hard to get to, huge and wild. The animal life is awesome: great bears, wolves, white mountain sheep, moose and caribou. A third of the way across the Pacific, Hawaii features Kilauea, the world's most active volcano, and Haleakala, the largest dead crater. Six thousand miles due east of Hawaii sits St. John in the Virgin Islands, a jewel of a tropical island with the meekest wildlife and mildest climate imaginable.

Mount McKinley rises 18,000 feet above the plain. Few other mountains on earth rise quite so high or so spectacularly from their bases.

Mt. McKinley National Park ALASKA

In 1957, the Denali Highway was completed, connecting the Alaskan road system to Mount McKinley National Park. With the forging of this link, it became possible to visit by automobile, from Fairbanks or Anchorage, some of the roughest, wildest, and most exciting country in North America. Visitors from other states can drive through Canada via the famous Alaska highway. It's a long, lonely trip, but safe. Mount McKinley Park, more than 3,000 square miles of mountains, glaciers and tundra, spreads mostly northward from the Alaska Range to within 250 miles of the Arctic Circle.

The outstanding sight of this wilderness is Mount McKinley itself, at 20,320 feet the highest peak on the continent. Though this ice-clad pink granite monster is shorter by 8,700 feet than Asia's Mount Everest, it thrusts up abruptly 17,000 feet from a broad plain. Few other mountains on earth stand so high above the base. To the north and east McKinley is framed by the massive Alaska Range, which includes many mountains over two miles high. These, together with the enormous glacier systems they support and the long inland trek, frustrated climbing parties for many years.

Mount McKinley's modern history began in 1896, when a sourdough guessed its height within a few hundred feet and named it after the Republican candidate for President (soon elected, then assassinated). In 1903 a certain Judge Wickersham led the first attempt on the twin-peaked mountain, but he chose to try the sheer north face, a tall, spectacular mountain wall, which still remains unclimbed.

In 1905 gold was discovered in nearby Kantishna River and a noisy gold camp sprang up. Now a ghost town, it makes an interesting side visit. It was two prospectors from the place, William Taylor and Pete Anderson, who in 1910 pioneered the "Muldrow Glacier Route" and climbed McKinley's 19,470-foot north peak. Their ascent, made with simple preparations and casual daring, is a classic in the annals of mountaineering. But it was not until 1913 that Hudson Stuck's party scaled the south peak, McKinley's true summit. For most climbing parties, McKinley's weather is a harsher enemy than the thin air or the climb itself. Vicious blizzards and blinding frozen fogs are constant hazards.

In winter, with the ghostly Northern Lights flickering overhead, temperatures of 20 and 30 below zero are not unusual. Though summer temperatures of 60 to 80 degrees set the tundra ablaze with brilliant flowers, intermittent permafrost lies below—deep-frozen, rock-hard earth that has not thawed for thousands of years.

Only a few birds—notably the ptarmigan, magpie, chickadee and gray jay—can survive the bitter winter. But with spring over 130 species come, many to nest in the spruce forests, the scrub brush and stunted willows that carpet the tundra. Among them are such exotic and far-ranging specimens as the golden plover from Hawaii, the long-tailed jaeger from the islands near Japan, and the European wheatear from Asia.

The park's mammals number 37 species, ranging from the mite-sized shrew to the moose which may weigh three-quarters of a ton. The Alaska moose is the largest member of the deer family. A large male might stand 7½ feet tall at the shoulders. Early in July thousands of caribou graze their way across the hillsides through their summertime feeding grounds. Tremendous grizzly bears shoulder through thickets and countryside, supplementing their plant diet with carrion and small animals. Red fox, Canada lynx, coyote and wolverine spend their winters constantly on the move, in search of a meager meal.

But by far the most interesting of the park's denizens are the Dall sheep, slightly smaller and finer boned than the Rocky Mountain bighorn, and the gray wolves, who live here in one of their last strongholds on the continent. Naturalist Adolph Murie has made a fascinating study of these two species and the complicated balance between them. His findings show that the wolves not only exert a useful control over the sheep

Timber wolves are making a last stand in Alaska. Like other wildlife, they are protected within park boundaries.

population, but also tend to improve the breed of sheep by culling out the weaklings.

The season at Mount McKinley, second largest of America's national parks, runs from June 1 to September 10, when there are 18 hours and more of daylight. There are comfortable accommodations at the McKinley Park Hotel. Visitors are urged to make reservations well in advance. Campers will find several campgrounds. However, firewood is scarce; a gas stove and plenty of warm gear are essentials. Hunting is forbidden, of course. Fishing, mainly for grayling, is good but carefully controlled. The park has 100 miles of gravel roads and several self-guiding trails.

Mt. McKinley National Park

SE Alaska. Area: 3,000 sq. mi.

Season: June 10-Sept. 10.

Climate: summer 60° to 80°.

Accommodations: hotel, camp and trailer sites.

Services: bus service in park, pack horses, fishing.

Park can be reached by car, via Alaska Highway and Denalo Highway, rail or air from Anchorage or Fairbanks.

Yellow flowers cover rocks at Sandy Cove, across the water from Muir Inlet.

Glacier Bay National Monument ALASKA

Hundreds of miles of rugged coastline, 3,600 square miles of mountain-choked wilderness, six peaks at least two miles high, dozens of mighty glaciers oozing downslope to end in massive white cliffs at the edge of branching tidal inlets—this is Glacier Bay National Monument, remote, difficult to get to, visited by few—a raw and superb piece of country.

Lying a half-hour by plane and a day by boat from Juneau, Alaska, Glacier Bay itself resembles the fjordlands of Norway and New Zealand, and is still being shaped by similar conditions. Moisture-laden ocean air, driven by storms that originate in the Aleutian Islands, sweep along Alaska's southeast coast. As the winds reach the St. Elias and Fairweather ranges, which frame the 50-mile length of the bay, the air rises and cools, dumping tremendous snowfalls on the inland heights. Here the snow melts, refreezes, and turns into ice by the pressure of its own weight. Millions of tons each year are fed into the monument's glacier systems. Seeking a lower level, the glaciers carry with them vast loads of rock and gravel. It is their grinding, gouging passage that has carved the fjordlike profile of Glacier Bay, that appears as we know it today.

Each glacier flows at its own speed. Most of them travel so slowly, however, that the famous Muir Glacier, whose lower end or snout is almost two miles wide and about 265 feet high, is by comparison racing along at 20 to 30 feet a day. Regardless of their rate of flow, most glaciers in the monument are currently in equilibrium: that is, their snouts remain stationary because snowfall in the mountains and melting in the lowlands balance each other. But this state is easily disrupted. In response to a period of unusually heavy snows, the glaciers advance, and during a particularly warm time their snouts retreat. Thus these enormous rivers of ice are remarkably sensitive indicators of short-term changes in weather.

Even more remarkable is the evidence these glaciers reveal of long-term changes in climate. The stumps of ancient trees, preserved for centuries under ice and only recently uncovered, leave no doubt that much of the region was densely forested during a warm-weather cycle, then completely leveled and buried by the vast glacial surge of a cold-weather cycle. Scientists estimate that around the year 1700 A.D. the whole of Glacier Bay lay under an ice cap more than a half-mile thick. Then a warming trend began. By 1890 the melting edge of ice had retreated about 20 miles, freeing the greater part of the bay. In 1899 a great earthquake joggled the region, speeding up the glaciers' flow. During the next 48 years, Muir Glacier withdrew over 13 miles. Today experts in weather and glaciers keep the bay under constant scrutiny, trying to determine whether the warming trend will continue or suddenly be reversed.

As the glaciers withdraw, they expose naked, rock-strewn earth. Before many years, however, primitive lichens and mosses reinvade the barren ground. These plants actually create soil out of rock, conditioning the area for more complicated vegetation—grasses, fireweed, alpine flowers. With the soil enriched by their decay, dwarf willows, then alders and cottonwood follow. At last, decades later, spruce and hemlock crowd out the thickets of lesser trees and spread the slopes with a mantle of dense, tall greenery.

As the plants multiply, grazing animals return to feed on them, and a few carnivores return to feed on the grazers. Today, much of the region formerly covered by ice is once more under forest, and mountain goats are common in the area. There are red fox, beaver, marten, mink, wolverine, and three kinds of bear—grizzly, black, and Alaska brown. The rocky shores make ideal roosts for gulls, ravens, ptarmigan, loons, and a profusion of waterfowl. Beyond, in sheltered stretches of the bay, hair seals ride on drifting floes, and an occasional whale can be seen among schools of porpoises.

Glacier Bay National Monument

SE Alaska. Area: 3,554 sq. mi.
Season: summer months.
Climate: mild in summer.
Accommodations: camp sites.
Park is 100 mi. by boat or air, from Juneau.

Katmai National Monument

(SEE PAGE 158)

SE Alaska. Area: 4,215 sq. mi.
Season: June 15-Oct. 1.
Climate: mild in summer.
Accommodations: tent camps, mess halls.
Services: sleeping bags, necessities.
Can be reached only by air from Anchorage, and bush plane from King Salmon.

Cakes of ice break off from the snout of Muir Glacier as it enters the waters across the bay.

Katmai National Monument

ALASKA

On June 6, 1912, the citizens of Juneau, Alaska, were disturbed by a deep rumble in the distance. They didn't know it at the time, but that rumble was Novarupta volcano exploding on the Alaska Peninsula, 750 miles due west across the Gulf of Alaska. Novarupta, near Mount Katmai, was one of the three greatest explosions ever recorded by man. About five cubic miles of volcanic debris were blasted into the air. Ash settled in a blanket three feet thick over the village of Katmai, 12 miles away, and ten inches thick over Kodiak Island, more than 100 miles away. For six months, fine dust in the stratosphere produced lurid sunsets over half the world and lowered temperatures as far away as North Africa.

The Katmai region was little known and inaccessible except by boat, and it wasn't until 1915 that expeditions began to arrive to study the site of the holocaust. It was learned that the natives, frightened by the first earthquakes, had fled the three nearest villages, never to return. All plant and animal life in the vicinity was destroyed. Mount Katmai collapsed: all that remained was a vast bowl-like crater eight miles in circumference. Today this is a lofty green lake about 500 feet deep. To the northwest spreads a sight just as spectacular. As Dr. Robert F. Griggs described it: "The whole valley as far as the eye could reach was full of hundreds, no, thousands–literally tens of thousands–of smokes curling up from its fissured floor." Thus was named the Valley of Ten Thousand Smokes, more than 40 square miles of once-lush bottom land that had been smothered under a 100-foot layer of foaming, glowing, swift-running lava which cooled into an expanse of glassy sands and white pumice stone.

Now fewer than ten of the many thousand vents still send up plumes of steam. Greenery has crept back to cover many of the volcanic scars, and wildlife has returned to the surrounding areas in abundance. The Alaskan brown bear, which weighs up to 1,800 pounds and is the world's largest carnivore, can be seen on summer days fishing swift rivers for red salmon. Giant moose lumber through six-foot-high reedgrass which thrives in this damp, subarctic place. Wolf, red fox, Canadian lynx, otter, beaver, and mink inhabit the white spruce forests which distinguish an adjacent life zone, technically called the Hudsonian landscape. Many species of waterbird nest along the bays and fjords of Shelikof Strait. The golden and the bald eagles wheel over the glaciers, waterfalls, snow-clad peaks, and deep blue lakes.

Good fishing may be had in Katmai's rugged wilderness.

Katmai, a national monument since 1916, contains more than two and a half million acres of the wildest kind of wilderness–some of the last land in the United States that remains untouched by the hand of man. You'll find no refreshment stands or comfort stations in Katmai, no roads into the Park, although a 23-mile jeep trail will be opened in 1963. A visit there will be a rewarding experience to those adventurous souls who like to go far from the beaten track. Commercial airlines fly to King Salmon terminal from Anchorage, 200 miles to the northeast. At King Salmon bush planes with pontoons can be hired to fly the 35 miles to Brooks River Camp within Katmai. Log cabin camps, each with mess hall, operate from the middle of June into October, when the weather is mild. They furnish sleeping bags and most necessities. For further information write to Northern Consolidated Airlines, in Anchorage, Alaska.

Hawaii Volcanoes National Park

HAWAIIAN ISLANDS

Far below the ocean floor the earth's crust shifted and faulted. Immense pressure from the earth's molten heart forced a gap in the weakened spot. Lava shot through the rupture, thrust upward to the ocean bed, and surged into the sea, a seething, superheated mass building higher and higher as the ocean depths boiled around it. Gradually, as new eruptions occurred, a mighty mountain was formed beneath the surface. Finally its peak emerged, steaming, above the waters of the blue Pacific.

That was roughly the way the Hawaiian Islands were formed, nearly 20 million years ago. That is what a geologist means when he says that these islands, and many others, especially in the Pacific ocean, are "of volcanic origin."

Two of Hawaii's islands display their volcanic pedigree so spectacularly that national parks have been established on them where visitors can get acquainted with Pacific geology at close quarters. On the largest island, Hawaii, is Hawaii Volcanoes National Park where famed Mauna Loa, a 13,680-foot volcano, puts on a stupendous spectacle of eruption on the average of once every three years.

Kilauea, unlike Mauna Loa, is a flattened dome with a collapsed center. Within this great caldera lies Halemaumau fire pit, an extraordinary lake of seething lava. During recent times the lava has overflowed onto the flat surrounding floor of Kilauea. Other times it drains away into the earth, producing avalanches of fiery rock along the fire pit's walls. A steam blast in 1924 enlarged Halemaumau to 3,000 feet in diameter and 1,300 feet deep. Since then it has partially re-filled.

Hawaii's volcanoes are predictable and tame, owing to the fluidity of their lavas. Earthquakes precede eruptions, then a crack opens up and the glowing, molten rock squirts into the air in great fountains. During a 1959 eruption of Kilauea Iki, near Kilauea crater, a fountain of lava reached a height of more than 1,000 feet, as tall as New York's Empire State Building! During a five-week period it filled the small crater with liquid lava 380 feet deep.

Kilauea Iki, near Mauna Loa on the island of Hawaii, erupted in 1959. Liquid lava fountains shot 1,900 feet high. Here, a frothy jet rises above nearby palm trees.

Amazing as these eruptions are, they are not dangerous. Other volcanoes cause people to flee in fear of their lives when they erupt, but Mauna Loa and Kilauea attract thousands of people from all over the world who come to witness the spectacular displays of their violent moods.

On the smaller island of Maui, 30 miles away, stands Haleakala, a dormant, 10,023-foot volcano whose 19-square-mile crater is one of the largest in the world and one of the showplaces of the national park system. It was originally an isolated section of Hawaii National Park. In 1961 it was established as a separate entity.

A boardwalk trail on the flank of Mauna Loa winds through a strange and alien landscape of skeletons of trees killed by showers of volcanic ash.

Pronounce it Hal-ee-ah-ka-LAH. Reach it by one of the inter-island airliners that link Honolulu to the rest of the state. You will land at Kahului Airport, on Maui, and drive from there to the park, taking a special touring car if you are a member of a party, or perhaps renting a car if you come alone.

A place to stay is important, for the best of this park—a trip into the crater—demands two or three days. But if you are hurried, drive up the winding surfaced road, past park headquarters, to the summit—the rim of the crater. There, spread before you, is a vast, cindery depression cut by two gaps, Koolau and Kaupo, where erosion wore away the crater walls. The crater floor, half a mile below you, is stippled with what appear to be ant

Haleakala crater, on the island of Maui is an ancient dead volcano. Within it are huts for overnight hikers.

Fern jungle, shaded by ohia trees, grows on Kilauea's northeast flank. Annual rainfall is more than 100 inches.

hills, rising from the black landscape. These are cinder cones, some nearly 1,000 feet tall, formed when volcanic activity within the old crater bestirred enough to blow holes in its floor.

On foot or horseback you may enter the crater and wander along its many trails. The Park Service maintains three cabins inside the bowl for the use of hikers and pack trips. Write beforehand to reserve your space. You can hire horses and a guide from Haleakala Crater Saddle Tours to take you there.

Silversword is an odd name. It refers to plants that grow nowhere else in the world but in the cinders of this crater. They are spherical clumps of metallic swordlike leaves, some a yard across, the baby ones the size of a ping-pong ball. Plumes of leaves rise vertically from those that are in bloom. Purple blossoms appear only once; then the plants die. Silverswords almost vanished during the 1920's because of depredations by wild goats and unrestrained human souvenir hunters. The park rangers have protected them and saved them from extinction.

Haleakala, at the time of writing, has no campground, though you may picnic at Hosmer Grove on the outer slope of the volcano. Many new facilities are to be established under the Mission 66 program.

Hawaii Volcanoes National Park

Hawaiian Islands. Area: 362 sq. mi.
Season: year round.
Climate: warm days, frequent showers, cool nights.
Accommodations: inns, campgrounds, cabins.
Services: visitor center, observatory, horses, trips.
Accessible by boat or air travel.

Eastward from St. Johns' Bordeaux Mountain, Fortberg Hill stands in Coral Bay; British Tortola rises in the distanc

Virgin Islands National Park VIRGIN ISLANDS

Three hundred years ago a ship that sailed near the West Indies kept a nervous lookout for pirates who might be waiting in any of a hundred coves or channels. This was the favorite place of Kidd and Blackbeard. This was the Spanish Main. It isn't likely the pirates had any idea that one of their island haunts would become a pleasure place.

Today, Virgin Islands National Park, occupying most of the heavenly isle of St. John, awaits all who may have dreamed of feeling trade winds, of knowing the waters of the buccaneers, of seeing the sort of refuge that sheltered the Brotherhood of the Coast, as the pirates called themselves.

Its more-than-probable use as a pirate base is only a small part of the history of this member of the Sugar Islands, which sailors have long called these mountainous links in the great chain of islands that form an arc between the United States and South America. More properly called one of the Lesser Antilles, St. John is about midway in that great sweep of landpieces 1,400 miles south southeast from New York, 900 miles southeast of Miami, and just east of Puerto Rico.

Nowadays, St. John is home for only a few thousand people, nearly all descendants of the slaves who worked its cane fields when plantations flourished there. It is likely that about the same number of warlike Indians, the Caribs, lived there in earlier centuries, too. What pirate activity occurred on its shores went on during the next hundred years. During that time, no honest men came to settle because of uncertainty as to what nation owned it. But in 1687, the Danes claimed it; and a few years later planters and soldiers

Two natives pause to chat on a St. John's country road.

landed under protection of the Danish flag. The settlers defied British claims to their island by building a fort, the ruins of which can still be seen.

By 1726, all its usable land was given over to plantations and a slave economy flourished. But if it was a very pleasant world for its planter overlords, it must have been the opposite for their slaves. They revolted in 1733, and for months kept the whites besieged on a neck of land now called Caneel Bay Plantation and the locale of sumptuous accommodations for tourists.

After the revolt was put down, slavery continued to be the basis for its prosperity until the mid-1800's, when it was abolished throughout the Danish West Indies.

The old estates could not be operated without free labor. First the planters and then most of the freed slaves departed; and then St. John gradually reverted to bush.

The United States became interested in the Virgin Islands after the Civil War, but not until 1917 did this country buy them from Denmark. By then, St. Thomas, St. Croix, and St. John were no longer the assets they had been for the Danes.

Meanwhile, word spread about the features of St. John: its white beaches, its mountains rising steep out of the sea up to 1,200 feet, its historical remains, its superb year-round climate with an average of 78 degrees, and its small but colorful population. Because of poor travel facilities, however, few people got to it, even though it is little more than a couple of miles from St. Thomas and 40 miles from St. Croix, which both became popular with tourists. But those who liked out-of-the-way places, with little care for fancy comfort, came back with glowing reports about its tranquility.

Among those who appreciated St. John was Laurance Rockefeller who made possible its preservation through the Jackson Hole Preserve Corporation, as a national park by contributing 5,000 acres to the government. Additional land was acquired and Congress authorized its establishment in the National Park system in 1956. Five thousand acres of offshore submerged lands were added by Act of Congress in October, 1962.

It can now be reached by regular launch service from St. Thomas where there is also an office for administration and information about it.

Do you have an image of an island in the South Seas? You may very well find St. John to be even an improvement on that dream. Here lofty palms wave in the soothing sea breezes. Here a terrain overhangs crescent beaches that can hardly be matched in the best the Pacific has to offer. There are no poisonous snakes and few mosquitoes. Game-fishing is excellent. Besides, it is thousands of miles closer to most of the United States than the islands of the South Seas. And its swimming is much pleasanter, owing to considerably warmer water.

In all, its natural treasures far exceed anything the pirates may have hidden in its sands. If their ghosts walk its beaches, no one would dream of reproaching them.

Virgin Islands National Park

St. John, V. I. Area: 19 sq. mi.

Season: year round.

Weather: tropical.

Accommodations: write Caneel Bay Plantation, 30 Rockefeller Plaza, N. Y. C., or Superintendent, V. I. National Park, St. John, V. I.

Index

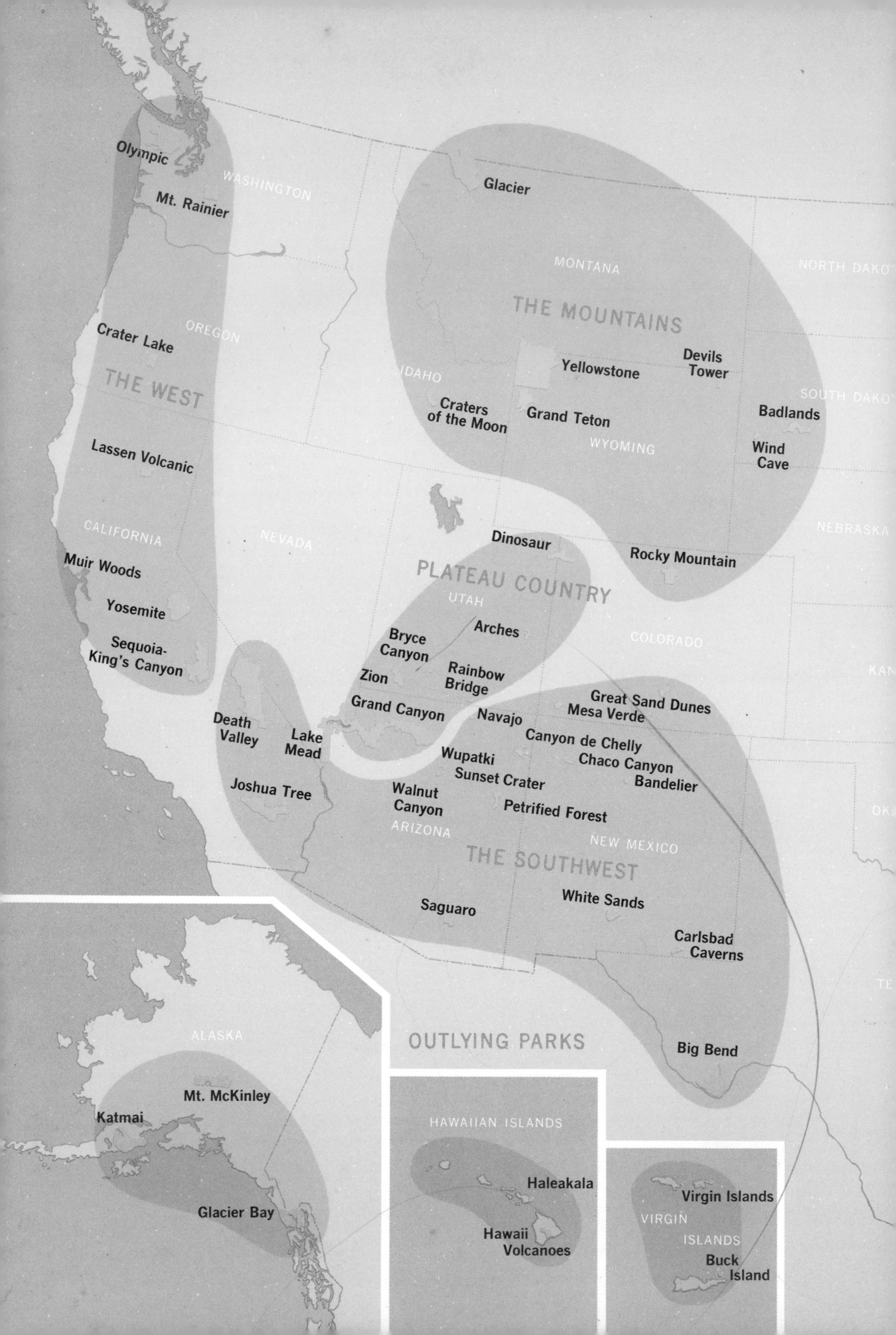
THE WEST
THE MOUNTAINS
PLATEAU COUNTRY
THE SOUTHWEST
OUTLYING PARKS
WASHINGTON
OREGON
CALIFORNIA
NEVADA
IDAHO
MONTANA
WYOMING
UTAH
COLORADO
ARIZONA
NEW MEXICO
NEBRASKA
Olympic
Mt. Rainier
Crater Lake
Lassen Volcanic
Muir Woods
Yosemite
Sequoia-King's Canyon
Glacier
Yellowstone
Devils Tower
Craters of the Moon
Grand Teton
Badlands
Wind Cave
Dinosaur
Rocky Mountain
Arches
Bryce Canyon
Zion
Rainbow Bridge
Grand Canyon
Death Valley
Lake Mead
Joshua Tree
Navajo
Great Sand Dunes
Mesa Verde
Canyon de Chelly
Chaco Canyon
Bandelier
Wupatki
Sunset Crater
Walnut Canyon
Petrified Forest
Saguaro
White Sands
Carlsbad Caverns
Big Bend
ALASKA
Mt. McKinley
Katmai
Glacier Bay
HAWAIIAN ISLANDS
Haleakala
Hawaii Volcanoes
VIRGIN ISLANDS
Virgin Islands
Buck Island